EXPERT DATABASE SYSTEMS A GENTLE INTRODUCTION

Paul Beynon-Davies

Senior Lecturer
Department of Computer Studies
Polytechnic of Wales, Pontypridd

McGRAW-HILL BOOK COMPANY

London · New York · St Louis · San Francisco · Auckland
Bogotá · Caracas · Hamburg · Lisbon · Madrid · Mexico · Milan
Montreal · New Delhi · Panama · Paris · San Juan · São Paulo
Singapore · Sydney · Tokyo · Toronto

Published by
McGRAW-HILL Book Company (UK) Limited
SHOPPENHANGERS ROAD · MAIDENHEAD · BERKSHIRE · ENGLAND
TEL: 0628 23432
FAX: 0628 35895

British Library Cataloguing in Publication Data

Beynon-Davies, Paul
    Expert database systems: a gentle introduction.
    1. Expert systems
    I. Title
    006.33

    ISBN 0-07-707240-5

Library of Congress Cataloging-in-Publication Data

Beynon-Davies, Paul.
    Expert database systems: a gentle introduction/Paul Beynon-Davies.
        p.   cm.
    Includes bibliographical references and index.
    ISBN 0–07–707240–5
    1. Expert systems (Computer science)   2. Data base management.
    I. Title.
QA76.76.E95B47   1991
006.3'3—dc20   90–36910
                                                                    CIP

1234   CUP   94321

Typeset by Computape (Pickering) Limited, Pickering, North Yorkshire
Printed and bound in Great Britain by the University Press, Cambridge

FOR RHYDIAN, CERI AND RHIANNON

Contents

Acknowledgements

Level5 is a product of Information Builders Inc.,
1250 Broadway, New York, NY 10001.

LEONARDO is a product of Creative Logic,
Brunel Science Park,
Uxbridge,
Middlesex UB8 3PQ.

GENERIS is a product of Deductive Systems Ltd,
Brunel Science Park,
Uxbridge,
Middlesex UB8 3PQ.

Foreword

When I was asked to become editor of this series I made the point to the publisher that commercial data processing is just another subdiscipline of software engineering. It is concerned with the development of large systems for particular application areas where requirements give rise to the storage of large amounts of data. This book nicely illustrates that point.

One of the most interesting phenomena of recent times has been the degree to which developments in commercial data processing foreshadow developments in other branches of software engineering. For example: commercial database-management systems rely on many of the ideas which form the basis of information hiding; fourth generation programming languages, particularly those associated with relational database systems, are merely an implementation of the idea of high-level data typing; and practitioners of commercial data processing were the first to point out the importance of requirements analysis. There is certainly a trend which seems to indicate that a technique or tool, which is used in commercial data processing, is used in other branches of software engineering a decade later.

This, I suspect, is true of expert database systems: they offer a high degree of flexibility and are an excellent medium for the encapsulation of the fuzzy requirements that we so often encounter at the beginning of a software project.

This timely book is an attempt to explain how an emerging artificial intelligence technology can be melded with a more mature commercial data-processing technology, in order to produce a technology which will be used to develop large systems in the 1990s.

If you work in the commercial data-processing area then you will find much that you can currently use. If you work in other areas of software engineering you will almost certainly find material in this book which will give you a decade start over your competitors.

Darrel Ince

ONE

Introduction

Some people believe Artificial Intelligence is the most exciting scientific and commercial enterprise of the century. Others raise distress flags, fearing eventual misuse. Still others scoff, arguing that the technology will come to nothing. One thing is clear however: Artificial Intelligence generates passion, and passion stimulates hyperbole-riddled rhetoric, and that rhetoric dangerously obfuscates. It is hard to tell if the field's promoters are pied-pipers leading us to the disappointment of excessive expectations or missionaries beckoning us to an almost inconceivable opportunity. (Winston and Prendergast, 1984)

The Primary Objective

This quote from the edited work by Winston and Prendergast sums up much of the contemporary discussion surrounding the discipline of artificial intelligence (AI). It sets the major question as being: is AI a field of exciting promise or simply a large white elephant doomed to eventual failure? There is, however, a major difficulty in answering this question, namely, that the tortuous jargon of the subject makes an informed decision all but impossible for the vast majority of people that matter. The people that matter are the people in business and industry who are looking for computing solutions to problems not well handled by the present generation of software. Unless they are awakened in some way to the potential of this new technology, then the question above will remain largely academic, in more than one sense of the word.

In this book we shall unravel some of the concepts of AI by studying in some detail one particular subdiscipline of this large and expanding field. That field is the development of knowledge base systems (KBS)—otherwise known as knowledge engineering. Knowledge base systems are chosen because they are probably the most tractable and practical products yet to emerge from AI. They are also the best examples of AI in

1

terms of the degree to which they have begun to receive commercial acceptance.

The primary aim of this book is therefore to give you, the reader, enough background knowledge to make an informed decision as to the relevance of AI in general and knowledge base systems in particular. The book is written for a number of people interested in this new venture. For example, software professionals interested in learning more about the subject, or students on computer science courses whose primary exposure is to conventional information systems—particularly those built around some form of database system. It is hoped that both such groups will benefit from the detailed discussion of the affinities between knowledge base systems and database systems presented here.

Themes

At the time of writing, many books on artificial intelligence, knowledge base systems, expert systems, and indeed database systems are available on the market. What then makes this book different from all the rest?

1. Although there are many books which provide a detailed discussion of each of these topics individually, there are few, if any, books which provide an introduction to the important integrative efforts taking place between these fields. Such efforts are usually encapsulated under the heading of expert database systems. It is an area that has been the focus of academic conferences with large and expensive published proceedings (Kerschberg, 1986; 1989). The present book makes this important material widely available in a more organized and inexpensive form.
2. The book takes a particularly pragmatic approach to the architecture of knowledge base systems. It makes the distinction between first- and second-order knowledge base systems—otherwise known as an evolutionary or revolutionary approach to the architecture of a KBS. First-order knowledge base systems are possible now through the integration of two sets of contemporary software: expert systems and database systems. Second-order knowledge base systems, which offer a more unified or 'orthogonal' approach to the problem of representing knowledge, are still very much a research endeavour.
3. The book is organized around the belief that artificial intelligence in general and knowledge base systems in particular have been subject to large amounts of unnecessary mystification. This introduction to

expert database systems attempts to demystify some of the key concepts in the area by emphasizing the practical application of knowledge base systems to industry. This primarily means basing the material around the extensive use of expert systems on small commercially oriented projects with a strong database flavour.

4. The author is firmly of the opinion that the distinction between software engineering and the new discipline of knowledge engineering has been overdone. In other words, that software engineering has much to offer knowledge engineering, and vice versa (Beynon-Davies, 1987). This emphasis comes out in the text in a number of senses. For instance, in the sense that knowledge base applications are likely to be increasingly incorporated not only into standard software applications, but also into the tools for building such applications (the so-called computer aided software engineering tools) (Beynon-Davies, 1989).

5. This book is largely the result of a final-year degree course taught by the author. In this course, great emphasis is placed on the case-study approach to learning. To give the book something of the flavour of this approach, two small case studies demonstrating the commercial application of expert database systems are discussed in Chapters 7 and 8.

An Imprecise Term

The term 'expert database system' has no precise meaning either for the academic computing world or for the computing industry. This is largely because the term is used to describe a gradually emerging, and constantly moving, research endeavour, rather than a developed software construct.

The present section, however, seeks to define at least some fuzzy boundaries for the expert database arena. It aims to provide an initial discussion of at least a range of possible definitions for the term by locating it within more established computing domains.

A study of the literature reveals at least four different interpretations defined by the intersection of larger and larger areas of computer science. In Fig. 1.1, these domains are portrayed as sets on a Venn diagram.

1. In its most limited sense the expert database domain can be defined as that endeavour which concerns itself with connecting together existing software tools such as database management systems and

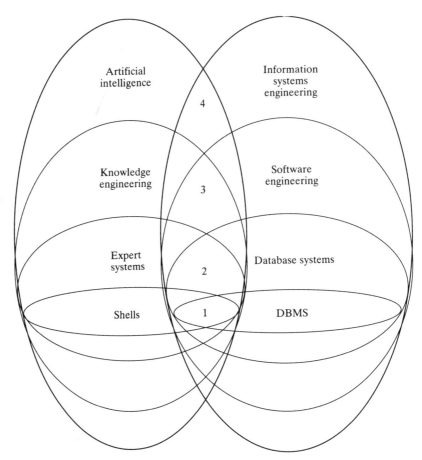

Figure 1.1.   Expert database systems definitions

expert system environments to solve problems at the fringes of conventional information processing. A great deal of discussion has taken place in recent times, for instance, concerning the value of expert system–database links as tools for constructing management information systems (Silverman, 1987).

2. In another sense the term expert database system is often used to describe the enhancement of data management systems with 'intelligent' software, or the enhancement of expert systems with more sophisticated data management facilities. Database systems are increasingly looking to expert systems technology to provide a necessary inferencing capability. Expert systems need databases to store the large amounts of facts needed by commercial applications (Stonebraker and Hearst, 1989).

3. The term expert database system is also used to cover most of the

advanced work in the database systems area. This is particularly true in a number of proposals for new database architectures such as semantic data models or the application of logic to database work. At this point people cease referring to the software under discussion as database software and start to refer to it as knowledge base software. In this sense we might define the field of expert database systems as the intersection of software engineering and knowledge engineering (Ullman, 1988; 1989).

4. Perhaps the most encompassing, but probably most controversial, definition of the term expert database system, however, would be any piece of software lying at the intersection of artificial intelligence work and information systems engineering work. Many of the most commercially successful offshoots of artificial intelligence would fall into this category (Reitman, 1984) including a growing number of computer aided software engineering tools which incorporate some degree of 'intelligence'.

Although there is disagreement about the precise nature of the term, the fundamental theme running through the work in the expert database area is the increasing convergence between many areas of computer science: expert system shells and database management systems, database systems and expert systems, knowledge engineering and software engineering, artificial intelligence and information systems development. This convergence revolves around a search for a more abstract and hence more encompassing level at which to build computer systems. This has been frequently referred to as the conceptual level. The fundamental problem in the development of all computer software is one of finding better and better methods of representing 'real-world' knowledge (Brodie *et al.*, 1984).

Limitations of the Book

It would be tempting for the author to choose the most limiting definition of the term 'expert database system' and concentrate on describing this area in some detail. This, however, would do an injustice to the field. It would not clearly reflect the other important interpretations represented in the literature. The author has therefore attempted to do justice to all the various interpretations of the term by providing an introductory overview of the field. We cannot claim therefore that the present book offers a comprehensive coverage of the field. We can claim that the book acts as a suitable bedrock for further investigation. To this end, a detailed list of further reading is provided at the end of the book.

Overview of the Book

We open our discussion with three chapters that define the boundaries of the expert database field. Chapter 2 reviews the historical development of database systems as probably one of the most successful types of software engineering tool to date. Chapter 4 seeks to establish a pragmatic definition of the discipline of artificial intelligence, knowledge base systems and expert systems. Chapter 3 acts as the first attempt to discuss the integration of expert system and database technology. In this chapter we consider a database system as a limited example of a knowledge base system and discuss how the concept of inference characteristic of expert systems is an important issue for the future development of database systems.

The remaining part of the book seeks to describe the intersection of AI and DB work in more detail. In Chapter 5 we make the distinction between first- and second-order expert database systems. The tripartite typology of first-order EDS discussed then serves to define the content of Chapters 6–8. Three of the most important second-order architectures are discussed in Chapters 9–11. We describe in Chapters 9 and 10 the attempt to construct even more meaningful models for data management. In Chapter 11 we provide an overview of the application of first-order logic in the realm of conventional and deductive database systems.

Chapter 12 concludes with a discussion of a suggested overarching framework for future computing activity—the idea of conceptual modelling. Conceptual modelling is a descriptive term for a central trend in the development of computer software—the idea that the history of computing is dominated by a central endeavour: the search for better methods of representing 'real-world' knowledge (Brodie *et al.*, 1984).

TWO

Database Systems

Introduction

Most of the software developed on the early business computers was developed in a piecemeal or *ad hoc* manner. Manual systems were analysed, redesigned and transferred onto the computer with little thought to their position within the organization as a whole.

The piecemeal approach by definition produces a number of separate information systems, each with its own program suite, its own files, and its own inputs and outputs. As a result, the systems by themselves do not represent the way in which the organization works, i.e., as a complex set of interacting and interdependent systems.

Because of the many problems inherent in the piecemeal approach, it is nowadays considered desirable to maintain a single centralized pool of organizational data, rather than a series of separate files. Such a pool of data is known as a database.

It is also considered desirable to integrate the systems that use this data around a piece of software which manages all interactions with the database. Such a piece of software is known as a database management system or DBMS.

Characteristics of Database Systems

A database may therefore be defined as a collection of structured data shareable between different parts of an organization's information system. A database is characterized by a number of properties:

1. Program–data independence. Databases, because of their sharing function, must be data-independent. Data independence might be defined as the immunity of applications to changes in the storage structure and access strategy of data (Date, 1986).

2. Data integration. This implies that a database should be a collection of data which has no unnecessarily duplicated or unused data (Howe, 1983).
3. Data integrity. This implies that when maintaining data we must be sure that no inconsistencies are likely to arise in the database.
4. Separate logical and physical views of data. One of the major ideas behind the database concept is embodied in the attempt to separate the business view of data from its physical representation on some device.

A database is an organized pool of shared data. A database management system or DBMS is a pool of shared facilities used to access and maintain a database. A DBMS acts as the interface between end-users, application programs and the database. It allocates storage, provides security and handles all the traditional demands of file processing.

A Brief History of Database Software

The history of database software dates back to the early 1960s when the first database systems were developed by individual companies to solve particular company problems. In the mid-1960s the first general-purpose packages became available. Perhaps the most famous of such packages was developed by the General Electric Company (GEC) called the integrated data store (IDS), originally designed to run specifically on GEC machines.

B. F. Goodrich saw the work that was being done at GEC and decided to port IDS across onto the new IBM system 360 range of computers. John Cullinane entered into a marketing agreement with Goodrich. This was the beginnings of a company named Cullinane, later Cullinet, which established the IDMS DBMS as the dominant force on IBM mainframes in the 1960s, 1970s and 1980s.

In 1969 a technical group operating under the auspices of CODASYL (Conference on Data Systems Languages) produced a specification of common database facilities which was strongly influenced by IDS and IDMS. The CODASYL model has been enhanced over the years to standardize the facilities of a range of DBMSs.

In 1970 an IBM scientist, Dr E. F. Codd, published an influential paper on database architecture (Codd, 1970). Researchers at IBM used the material in Codd's early publications to build the first prototype relational DBMS called system/R. This was emulated at a number of academic institutions, perhaps the foremost example being the INGRES research team at the University of Berkeley, California (Stonebraker, 1986).

During the 1970s and early 1980s relational databases got their primary support from academic establishments. The commercial arena was still dominated by IDMS-type databases. In 1983, IBM announced its first relational database for large mainframes—DB2. Since that time, relational databases have grown from strength to strength.

Data Models

All database software is built on an underlying data model. A data model is a general architecture for data organization. In terms of contemporary commercial acceptance, there are generally held to be three fundamental database models (see Fig. 2.1) (Tsitchizris and Lochovsky, 1982):

1. The hierarchical model is a direct extension of commonly used file-processing methods. Basically, data is organized hierarchically in relationships of ownership. For example, in an educational database, departments might be said to 'own' courses, which in turn 'own' students. The major problem with this approach is that it encourages data redundancy. Hence, in our example, if a number of departments collaborated in running a course, the course information would have to be duplicated for each participating department.

2. The network (CODASYL) model. This extends the concept of hierarchy into the concept of a network. Each entity or record within the database is joined to other relevant entities by a system of pointers. Using our educational example again, the three departments, three courses, and three students represented in Fig. 2.1 are linked together in a complex network. The major problem with the network model is that the programmer or end-user needs to know a great deal about how to 'navigate' through the database to extract information (Bachmann, 1973).

3. The relational model. The relational model organizes data in one uniform representation. Everything in a relational database is represented in the form of two-dimensional tables related together by common attributes.

    Probably because of its 'orthogonal' nature, the relational data model has attained some supremacy in recent times. It is for this reason that we devote the rest of this chapter to examining this data model in more detail.

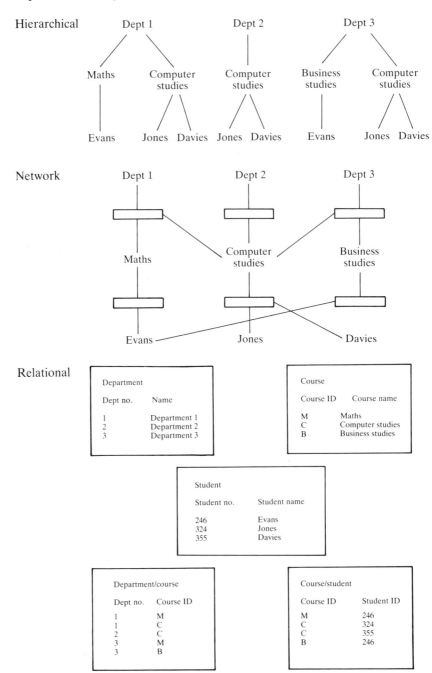

Figure 2.1. Data models

The Relational Data Model

Codd has always maintained that there were three problems that he wanted to address with his theoretical work:

1. Codd wanted to directly enhance the concept of program–data independence.
2. Codd maintained that prior data models treated data in an undisciplined fashion. His model was proposed as a disciplined way of handling data using the rigour of mathematics.
3. Codd wanted to improve programmer productivity. In 1982, when Codd received the ACM Turing award, the title of his acceptance paper was 'Relational Database: a practical foundation for productivity'.

The relational data model, just like any other data model, consists of three primary components (Codd, 1985):

1. A collection of data structures
2. A collection of operators
3. A collection of inherent integrity rules.

Let us examine each of these in turn.

Relational Data Structures

There is only one data structure in the relational data model: the table or relation. The rows of such tables are generally referred to as tuples, because the term has a generally more precise definition than row or record. Likewise, columns are usually referred to as attributes of the relation.

A relation is a disciplined table. Relations are tables constrained in the following way (Fig. 2.2):

1. All entries in a column must be of the same kind. They must come from the same 'domain'.
2. All columns must be assigned distinct names.
3. The ordering of columns is not significant.
4. Each row in a relation must be distinct. That is, duplicate rows are not allowed in any one relation.
5. Each column–row intersection (cell) in a relation should contain a single value. This is often referred to as an 'atomic' value. In other words, multiple values are not allowed in any one cell.

6. The ordering of rows is not significant.

EMPLOYEES_*Relation name*			
		Attributes	
Employee_no	Name	Position	Salary
01	Jones	project manager	20000 –
03	Brown	analyst/programmer	15000 – :
02	Smith	project manager	25000 *Tuples*
04	Stevens	systems manager	40000 – :
06	King	project manager	25000 – :
05	Harris	programmer	10000 –

Figure 2.2. A simple relation

The constraint detailed above, that each row must be distinct, means that each relation must have a so-called primary key. That is, an attribute or combination of attributes whose value or values uniquely identify the rows. A relation may also contain so-called foreign keys, i.e., keys that reference other relations in a database.

The important point, however, is that interconnection between data in a relational database is represented in one and only one way—through attributes from a common domain. Hence in Fig. 2.3, there is a clear relationship between the EMPLOYEES and PROJECTS table represented by the attribute PROJECT_NO in the EMPLOYEES table and the attribute NUMBER in the PROJECTS table. Although the attributes are named differently, they are defined on a common domain. By this we mean that the values for the attribute PROJECT_NO are taken from the same delimited set of values available to the NUMBER attribute in the PROJECTS table.

EMPLOYEES				
Employee_no	Name	Position	Salary	Project_no
01	Jones	project manager	20000	01
03	Brown	analyst/programmer	15000	01
02	Smith	project manager	25000	02
04	Stevens	systems manager	40000	
06	King	project manager	25000	02
05	Harris	programmer	10000	02

PROJECTS			
Number	Description	Start	Estimated_end
01	payroll	01/01/89	01/01/91
02	stock control	01/01/88	01/01/91

Figure 2.3. A simple relational database

It is frequently useful to refer to the structure of a relation independently of its actual tuples—an intensional rather than an extensional definition. This is usually done by defining a relation using some form of bracketing notation. For example,

⟨relation name⟩ (⟨attribute name⟩, ⟨attribute name⟩, . . .)

It is also common practice to underline the primary key of the relation. For instance,

EMPLOYEES (employee—no, name, position, salary, project—no)

Relational Algebra

One of the distinguishing characteristics of the relational model as opposed to the hierarchical or network model is that the manipulative part of the relational model is designed to operate on whole files (relations) of data, rather than on the individual records (tuples) or fields (attributes) within a file. The manipulative part of the relational model consists of a set of operators known collectively as the relational algebra. The result of any retrieval operation in the relational algebra is always another relation. Each operation takes either one or two relations as its operands and produces a new relation as a result. The three fundamental operators of the relational algebra are:

1. Selection. Creates a subset of all rows in a table (Fig. 2.4).

```
SELECT FROM EMPLOYEES WHERE SALARY ≥ 20000 → HIGH_SALARIES

HIGH_SALARIES

Employee_no   Name     Position           Salary   Project_no
01            Jones    project manager    20000    01
02            Smith    project manager    25000    02
04            Stevens  systems manager    40000
06            King     project manager    25000    02
```

Figure 2.4. An example of selection

2. Projection. Creates a subset of all columns in a table (Fig. 2.5).

```
PROJECT NAME, POSITION, PROJECT_NO FROM EMPLOYEES → POSITIONS

Name       Position             Project_no
Jones      project manager      01
Brown      analyst/programmer   01
Smith      project manager      02
Stevens    systems manager
King       project manager      02
Harris     programmer           02
```

Figure 2.5. An example of projection.

3.   Join. Combines two tables on a common column (Fig. 2.6).

```
JOIN POSITIONS AND PROJECTS ON PROJECT_NO → RESULT

RESULT

Name    Position              Project_no  Description    Start       Estimated end

Jones   project manager       01          payroll        01/01/89    01/01/91
Brown   analyst/programmer    01          payroll        01/01/89    01/01/91
Smith   project manager       02          stock control  01/01/88    01/01/91
King    project manager       02          stock control  01/01/88    01/01/91
Harris  programmer            02          stock control  01/01/88    01/01/91
```

Figure 2.6.   An example of a join.

Figures 2.4–2.6 demonstrate the application of some statements in the relational algebra on the tables in Fig. 2.3. As well as the three fundamental operations of selection, projection and join, a number of other operators have been identified:

4.   Union. Adds two tables together.
5.   Difference. Subtracts two tables.
6.   Intersection. Creates a table with common rows.
7.   Divide. Divides a table having two columns with a table having one column.

The Relational Calculus

The relational calculus represents an alternative to the relational algebra as a candidate for the manipulative part of the relational model. It is important here primarily because of its strong associations with a branch of logic known as the predicate calculus to be discussed in Chapter 11.

The difference between the relational algebra and the relational calculus is as follows. In the relational algebra the user specifies the detailed procedures for extracting information. In the relational calculus the user defines what he wants, leaving the database system to work out the procedure required. In this sense the algebra can be said to be procedural whereas the calculus is non-procedural or declarative.

An expression in the relational calculus has two parts:

1.   A target list which consists of an inventory of the required elements, separated by commas
2.   A logical expression, called a predicate, which defines the wanted

elements in terms of the relations from which they are to be extracted.

A relational calculus expression is therefore written as:

$$\langle \text{Target List} \rangle \quad \text{WHERE} \quad \langle \text{predicate} \rangle$$

This may be interpreted as 'extract the elements in the target list such that the predicate is true.' For example, the expression:

```
employees.employee_no, employees.project_no
WHERE EXISTS
temp(temp.employee_no = employees.employee_no AND
     temp.project_no = 01)
```

would extract all employees on project 01.

Integrity rules

Integrity refers to the accuracy or correctness of data in a database. It normally means protecting the database from authorized users by the application of some set of rules which are designed to maintain the logical consistency of the database. Because of the importance of this topic we shall devote a substantial amount of attention to this issue in Chapter 3. Suffice it to say here that, in relational databases, two such rules are of primary importance.

1. Entity integrity refers to the rule that in any relation there must always be a primary key, and that no part of the primary key may be null, i.e., not exist. What we are really saying here is that there must always be a unique identifier for each row in a table. Each employee for instance must be uniquely identified via an employee_no.
2. Referential integrity refers to the rule that states a foreign key must either be null or the value of the primary key of an associated table. The reasoning behind this rule is as follows: if a row of relation EMPLOYEES contains a foreign key PROJECT_NO, then a row for the project should exist in relation PROJECTS. If the foreign key is null, then we must be certain that no row corresponding to PROJECT_NO exists in PROJECTS.

A Relational Database Management System

In the above discussion we have described some of the components that go into defining the characteristics of a relational database. Of equal importance, however, is that piece of software which manages all interaction with the database by end-users and application programs—the so-called relational database management system (RDBMS).

Many of the characteristics of an RDBMS have already been discussed in terms of DBMSs in general. All we shall say here is to reiterate that one of the primary goals of any DBMS is to achieve something called program–data independence—the necessary separation of data from the application programs that use it. This facility is important in the sense that it allows us to evolve our database without worrying about the impact that such evolution might have on our application programs. For example, an RDBMS should allow you to add a new column to a table, change the format of a data item, or even add a new table to the database without the need to change any of the software that accesses the database.

There are a number of ways in which program–data independence is achieved in an RDBMS. Most such mechanisms, however, revolve around the use of an entity known as the system catalogue, database catalogue, database directory or data dictionary. In essence, the system catalogue is the place where all the table definitions for a particular system reside. Hence, a primitive system catalogue for the projects database presented earlier might look as follows:

TABLES			COLUMNS			
Tabname	Colcount	Creator	Tabname	Colname	Type	Len
employees	4	PBD	employees	employee_no	char	2
projects	3	PBD	employees	name	char	20
			employees	position	char	20
			employees	salary	num	10
			employees	project_no	num	2
			projects	number	num	2
			projects	description	char	20
			projects	start	date	
			projects	estimated_end	date	

The system catalogue encourages program–data independence in that any changes made to the structure of the database are made to the system catalogue, not to the data itself. Hence, we should be able to change the length of the employee_no attribute without affecting programs which access the employees table.

A Cook's Tour of SQL

One of the major formalisms which define the present generation of relational database management products is Structured Query Language or SQL for short. SQL is fundamentally a query language based on the relational calculus, and thus inherits the nonprocedural strengths of the calculus. SQL, however, is a lot more than simply a query language—Codd refers to it as a database sublanguage. It is becoming the standard interface to relational and nonrelational DBMS.

SQL comes in three major parts:

1. A data definition language (DDL)
2. A data manipulation language (DML)
3. A data control language (DCL).

In the following pages we shall provide a tutorial guide to SQL.

Data Definition Language

Suppose that we have a company requirement to produce a database of information (Fig. 2.7). The structure for each of the tables in the database can be set up using the create table command. For example:

```
CREATE TABLE  (table name)
       ((attribute name) (type) ((length)),
           ...              ...      ...,
           ...              ...      ...)

CREATE TABLE SALES
       (sales_no char (4),
        product_no char (4),
        customer_no char (4),
        qty number (3))
```

The create table statement allows us to specify a name for a table, and the names, data-types and lengths of each of the attributes in the table. SQL, however, has no direct mechanism for enforcing the notion of primary and foreign keys.

Most implementations of SQL currently recognize only two ways of implementing integrity: UNIQUE in the CREATE INDEX statement, and NOT NULL in the CREATE TABLE statement. Both such mechanisms are designed to implement the notion of entity integrity. For instance, suppose we create a table of sales information as above, but this time add a clause to one of the attribute definitions:

```
CREATE TABLE SALES
       (sales_no char (4) NOT NULL,
        product_no char (4),
        customer_no char (4),
        qty_ordered number (3));
```

```
SALESFORCE

Salesman_no  Salesman_name  Sales_area  Sales_target

01           Jones  S        Cardiff     2000
03           Jenkins  P       Valleys     1500
02           Thomas  J        Newport     1700
04           Davies  A        Swansea      600

CUSTOMERS

Customer_no  Customer_name            Sales_area

01           Friendly Foods           Cardiff
03           Rookem Insurance         Newport
02           Dodgy Videos             Valleys
04           Crap Cars                Swansea
06           Raunchy Restaurants      Valleys

SALES

Sales_no  Product_no  Customer_no  Qty

1004      014         03           20
2053      014         02           40
1342      028         04           30
1556      028         06           50
2555      014         06           30

PRODUCTS

Product_no  Product_description  Supplier_no

014         Wonderful Widget     1432
032         Sticky Stationery    2468
028         Stampy Stapler       3521
056         Bandy Binder         2468

STOCK

Product_no  Qty_in_Stock  Re_order Level

014         200           30
032         300           50
028         250           40

SUPPLIERS

Supplier_no  Supplier_name        Sup_address  Sup_tel

1432         Widgets Inc.         Crosby       246832
2468         Standard Stationery  Leeds        438127
3521         Standard Staplers    London       381766
```

Figure 2.7.   The sales database

The declaration NOT NULL in this statement declares sales‗no to be the primary key of the SALES table. Unfortunately, however, although users are now always required to enter a value for the primary key, they are able to enter as many duplicate values for sales‗no as they like. This clearly infringes the uniqueness condition of a primary key. To enforce the uniqueness condition the DBA has to create an index on sales‗no as follows:

```
CREATE UNIQUE INDEX sales_ind ON sales (sales_no);
```

Unlike entity integrity, SQL does not presently have any means for specifying referential integrity. In the short term, however, it is expected that a number of extensions will be made to the standard to incorporate both referential integrity and a more satisfactory means of implementing entity integrity.

When an index or a table is created information is written to a number of system tables. This is a meta-database, if you like, which stores information about the structure of tables at the base level. Information about a table or an index can be removed from the system tables by using the DROP command:

```
DROP TABLE ⟨table name⟩

DROP INDEX ⟨index name⟩ ON ⟨table name⟩

DROP INDEX sales_ind ON sales

DROP TABLE sales
```

Only a certain amount of amendment activity is allowed on table structures by SQL. We can add an extra attribute to a table:

```
ALTER TABLE ⟨table name⟩
ADD (⟨attribute name⟩ ⟨attribute type⟩ (⟨attribute length⟩))

ALTER TABLE employees
ADD (eyecolour char (8))
```

We can also modify the size of an existing attribute:

```
ALTER TABLE ⟨table name⟩
MODIFY (⟨attribute name⟩ ⟨attribute type⟩ (⟨new length⟩))

ALTER TABLE employees
MODIFY (job char (20))
```

Table Maintenance

Having created a structure for the tables in our database, we can enter data into such tables using the INSERT command:

```
INSERT INTO ⟨table name⟩
(attribute1_name, attribute2_name,...)
VALUES
('value1', 'value2',...)

INSERT INTO Customers
(customer_no,name,area)
VALUES
(01, 'Friendly Foods', 'Cardiff')
```

If the list of values is in the same sequence as the sequence of attributes in the table, the sequence of attribute names can be omitted:

```
INSERT INTO ⟨table name⟩
VALUES
('value1', 'value2',...)

INSERT INTO Customers
VALUES
(01, 'Friendly Foods', 'Cardiff')
```

We can also maintain the ongoing data in the database through use of the update and delete commands:

```
UPDATE ⟨table name⟩
SET ⟨attribute1 name⟩ = ⟨new value⟩
    ⟨attribute2 name⟩ = ⟨new value⟩
    ...
WHERE ⟨condition⟩

UPDATE Customers
SET Sales_area = 'Valleys'
WHERE Customer_no = '01'

DELETE FROM ⟨table name⟩
WHERE ⟨condition⟩

DELETE FROM Customers
WHERE Customer_no = '01'
```

Retrieval

Although SQL has a data definition and file maintenance subset, the language was designed primarily as a means for extracting data from a database. Such extraction is accomplished through use of the select command: a combination of the select, project, and join operators of the relational algebra.

Simple retrieval is accomplished by a combination of the select, from and where clauses:

```
SELECT ⟨attribute1 name⟩, ⟨attribute2 name⟩, . . .
FROM ⟨table name⟩
WHERE ⟨condition⟩

SELECT employee_no, name, job
FROM employees
WHERE job = 'Analyst'
```

The list of attribute names can be substituted with the wildcard character '*', in which case all the attributes in the table are listed:

```
SELECT *
FROM employees
WHERE job = 'Analyst'
```

To produce a sorted list as output we add the order by clause to the select statement:

```
SELECT employee_no, name, job, salary
FROM employees
WHERE job = 'Analyst'
ORDER BY salary
```

The default order is ASCII ascending. To produce the list in descending order we add the keyword DESC.

```
SELECT employee_no, name, job, salary
FROM employees
WHERE job = 'Analyst'
ORDER BY salary DESC
```

To undertake aggregate work such as computing the average salary of employees in a particular department we use the GROUP BY clause:

```
SELECT deptno, avg(sal), count (*)
FROM employees
WHERE deptno IN (10,20)
GROUP BY deptno
```

Note the use of the IN operator to specify a range of matchable values.

The structure in SQL originally referred to the ability to nest queries in select statements. For instance, to find out who makes more money than Jones we would write:

```
SELECT employee_no, name
FROM employees
WHERE salary )
     (SELECT salary
      FROM employees
      WHERE name = 'JONES')
```

SQL evaluates the innermost query first. This produces a result which is compared with the result produced from the outermost query.

SQL performs relational joins by indicating common attributes in the where clause of a select statement. For instance, the select statement below extracts data from the salesforce and customers tables of relevance to salesman working in the Valleys sales area, and orders it by the salesman_no attribute.

```
SELECT salesman_no, salesman_name, customer_no, customer_name
FROM salesforce, customers
WHERE salesforce.sales_area=customers.sales_area
AND customers.sales_area='Valleys'
ORDER BY salesman_no
```

Data Control Language

The primary mechanism for enforcing integrity issues in SQL is through the concept of a view. Views are virtual tables which act as 'windows' in on the database composed of real tables. The view below establishes a virtual table for use by salesmen working in the Valleys sales area. Such salesmen granted access only to this view would be unable to see information of relevance to other sales areas in the company's sales profile.

```
CREATE VIEW VALLEYS
AS SELECT Customer_no, Customer_name, Sales_no, Product_no, Qty
FROM Sales, Customers
WHERE Sales.Customer_no=Customers.Customer_no
  AND Sales_area='Valleys'
```

This view defines limited access for users on all customers in the Valleys area. This view becomes a table definition in the system catalogue and remains unaffected by changes in the underlying SALESFORCE table.

Access can be restricted on tables and views to particular users via the GRANT and REVOKE facilities of SQL. GRANT allows users read and file maintenance privileges on tables or views. REVOKE takes such privileges away.

```
GRANT SELECT ON sales TO pbd

GRANT INSERT, UPDATE
ON customers
TO pbd

REVOKE SELECT, INSERT
ON customers
FROM pbd
```

Future Trends

Relational database systems have been seen to be the bedrock of much future computing activity. For instance, RDBMSs are seen by many to be the logical first step in building distributed database systems and knowledge-based systems.

A distributed database might be defined as the union of a set of databases held at different locations. RDBMSs are seen as being of primary importance in this area because of their ability to handle data fragmentation—that is, the ability of a DBMS to transparently combine sets of information held at various remote sites into a coherent single picture for the end-user. This is possible in an RDBMS because of its underlying simple unitary data structure. In traditional CODASYL-type databases the problems of unifying a multitude of complex data structures makes distribution a much more difficult task (Date, 1986).

Many existing RDBMS products benefit from the use of artificial intelligence techniques in such areas as query optimization, memory management, and natural language interfaces. Given that the relational approach has a sound theoretical basis in predicate logic, however, natural connections have been made with the whole area of logic programming and knowledge-based systems.

Problems

1. What are the primary properties of a database system?
2. What are the primary components of a data model?
3. What makes a table different from a relation?
4. What are entity and referential integrity?
5. Use SQL to define the structure of the EMPLOYEES table in Fig. 2.3.
6. Using the two-table database in Fig. 2.3, write SQL retrieval statements for the following enquiries:
    (a) give me the employee record for Jones;
    (b) give me a list of project numbers;
    (c) what is the salary of employee number 04?
    (d) give me the names of everybody on the Payroll project;
    (e) give me the average salary of people on each project.
7. Compare and contrast SQL with the relational algebra.

THREE

Information, Knowledge and Inference

Introduction

Relational databases store facts about the objects in a 'real-world' domain and some primitive information about the relationships between such objects. For instance, in the projects example described in the previous chapter, the database represents two objects, namely an EMPLOYEE and a PROJECT. An EMPLOYEE is related to a PROJECT in the following way: EMPLOYEES are assigned to one PROJECT per EMPLOYEE, but a PROJECT may be made up of a collection of EMPLOYEES. Such a relationship between objects is said to be a one-to-many relationship: one PROJECT to many EMPLOY-EES (this form of modelling will be discussed in more detail in Chapter 12).

Facts about the 'real world' can hence be considered either as classifications of objects, or as representing relationships between objects (Israel, 1986). For example, Peter, John, Ann and Fred can be thought of as objects. They can be assigned to the class PERSON. Similarly, we can define relationships between objects. For instance, John and Peter may be involved in a management relationship—John manages Peter.

Relational databases represent objects as tables and relationships by values stored in tables. Hence, in a table of employee records we might have a field detailing the personnel number of an immediate superior. For instance,

```
employees (employee_no, name, address, manager_no)
```

This is in fact a recursive relationship between objects since manager_no, the foreign key, is taken from the same domain as employee_no.

Databases are however particularly ineffective at representing other important aspects of knowledge—namely rules.

Rules are important because they enable us to specify how to infer new instances of a class of objects, or new instances of a relationship, from previously unclassified objects. For example, suppose we have the following rule which applies to our enterprise:

```
IF PERSON_A manages PERSON_B
   AND PERSON_B manages PERSON_C
THEN PERSON_C reports-to PERSON_A
```

This simple rule specifies a piece of common-sensical knowledge. It allows us to deduce the fact, for instance, that Fred reports-to John from the following facts:

```
Peter manages John
John manages Ann
Ann manages Fred
```

In other words, IF John manages Ann AND Ann manages Fred THEN Fred reports-to John.

Facts and Rules

Knowledge can be represented as both facts and rules. Facts are frequently called declarative knowledge because they declare the relationships between objects. Rules are frequently called procedural knowledge because they define the process by which new facts are generated from old facts.

Database management systems are engines for handling large collections of facts. Rules can be represented but only in a declarative manner. For instance, the reports-to rule can be represented by storing values in another table which records the reporting relationship. Doing this for each such rule in our organization, however, would mean our having tables to represent all possible associations between objects.

Rules are hence primarily mechanisms for managing the 'information explosion' inherent in any attempt to represent reality. They are a more concise way of representing reality.

Knowledge base systems are traditionally engines for handling large collections of rules. To understand this, it is useful to make the distinction between procedural and declarative knowledge and a procedural and declarative representation for such knowledge. Procedural knowledge is traditionally represented in a procedural manner as high-level language code. What knowledge base systems are attempting to do, however, is in a sense to treat procedural knowledge, like the reports-to function, as stored data—i.e., to store it in a declarative representation. This knowledge will then be activated by a separate general-purpose processor which will perform all the appropriate inferencing in any particular case.

Advantages of Declarative Knowledge

The advantage of representing knowledge declaratively is that it makes for easier maintenance. Adding a rule to a knowledge base is a relatively simple matter; incorporating an additional rule into a section of COBOL code is not—it normally involves modifying the whole program.

The process of modifying a rule in a knowledge base is also straightforward. As we shall see in the next chapter, it involves either adding or deleting a condition, or adding or deleting a conclusion. Modifying the processing of a traditional program is a far different matter.

In a sense, the attempts made to design traditional commercial systems as a set of independent but interacting modules is an attempt to emulate many of the features of the declarative approach we have been discussing (Yourdon and Constantine, 1979). The modular design of systems is an attempt to handle functionality in procedure-like chunks which emulate rules in our knowledge base.

Representing knowledge declaratively enables knowledge to be in some sense modular or independent of the process which uses it. Moving on from our discussion of program–data independence, we might call this an example of knowledge–process independence.

Inference

Another important architectural difference between a knowledge base system and a conventional information system is the separation of inference and knowledge.

The word inference is derived from the Latin words 'in' and 'ferre' meaning 'to carry or bring'. Inference is therefore the process of bringing or carrying forward old knowledge into new knowledge. In our example above, the old knowledge represented by our collection of facts is turned into new knowledge, a new fact, by the application of inference; in our case the application of a rule.

Every computer system has an inferencing capability or inference 'engine'. In a conventional system, written say in a procedural language such as COBOL, the inference engine is represented by those parts of the program code that control the processing of the system. A conventional program or system has a limited inference capability that is totally intertwined with the knowledge it has to process.

In a knowledge base system, the knowledge is separated out from the inferencing mechanism. The inference engine in a knowledge base system is therefore a program which accesses not only data as in a conventional system, but also pieces of procedural knowledge as well.

In many ways this separation of inference and knowledge makes the process of system development that much easier. In developing a conventional system, the software engineer has to detail both the 'what' and the 'how': what the system is required to do, and how it is expected to do it. The development of a knowledge base system moves closer to the ideal of requiring the developer simply to specify the 'what', i.e., to declare what rules and facts are needed in the system. He can to a large extent ignore the question of how this knowledge is to be made to work or to be inferenced.

Database Integrity

To highlight some of the points made in the discussion above, we now consider database integrity as a problem of knowledge representation. We discuss how conventional relational database systems currently approach the knowledge representation problem, and also examine some proposals as to how they aim to approach this problem in the relatively near future.

First, let us review the notion of database integrity. A database is designed to record data of interest to some enterprise. To be of use to the enterprise, the data must be valid. Integrity is the problem of ensuring that the database contains only valid data.

In defining integrity it is useful to make the analogy with human relationships. When we say that a person has integrity, it usually means that we can believe what the person says. We trust the person's word. We use the word integrity in much the same way when we apply it to a database. If a database has integrity, then we believe it accurately reflects reality. We can trust it.

The task faced by the company data analyst or database administrator (DBA) is to discover the rules that govern data validity. The task is to find what business rules (sometimes referred to as constraints) determine what is, and what is not, valid data, and incorporate such rules into the design of a database.

Integrity then refers to the accuracy or correctness of data in a database. In contrast with database security, which might be defined as protecting the database from unauthorized access, database integrity normally means protecting the database from authorized users by the application of some set of rules designed to maintain the logical consistency of the database.

Relational Integrity

In relational databases two integrity rules are of primary importance: entity integrity and referential integrity as discussed in the previous chapter.

The traditional way of implementing integrity in conventional information systems is through a large amount of 3GL code. Increasingly, however, people, particularly in the relational database area, have discussed integrity mechanisms as desirable functions to place somewhere within the realms of a relational database management system. This is particularly true of the range of modern interfaces to RDBMS, of which SQL has emerged as the standard.

Most current implementations of SQL recognize only two ways of implementing integrity: UNIQUE in the CREATE INDEX statement, and NOT NULL in the CREATE TABLE statement. Both such mechanisms are designed to implement the notion of entity integrity discussed in Chapter 2.

Extensions to SQL

Unlike entity integrity, most implementations of SQL do not presently have any means for specifying referential integrity. In the short term, however, it is expected that a number of extensions will be made to incorporate both referential integrity and a more satisfactory means of implementing entity integrity.

Rather than having to specify the NOT NULL and UNIQUE conditions directly as above, future versions of SQL may incorporate a PRIMARY KEY function like the following:

```
CREATE TABLE SALES
    (sales_no char (4),
     product_no char (4),
     customer_no char (4),
     qty_ordered number (3))
    PRIMARY KEY (sales_no);
```

Simplifying matters a little, entity integrity concerns primary keys while referential integrity concerns foreign keys. When an update is attempted on a table containing a foreign key and that update violates a referential integrity constraint, two courses of action are possible:

1. reject the update and leave the database unchanged;
2. force through additional updates to achieve a database state that conforms to the constraints.

For each foreign key in the database, therefore, rules can specify which action to take in the case of an insert, delete or replace operation.
Consider, for instance, the following SQL query:

```
DELETE
FROM suppliers
WHERE supplier_no = '10';
```

The referential integrity constraint between suppliers and shipments can be met by any one of three actions:

1. Restrict. Disallow the deletion if any shipments records exist for supplier_no '10'.
2. Nullify. Set to null any supplier_no = '10'.
3. Delete. Delete any product record where supplier_no = '10'.

Any extension to SQL must therefore allow the DBA to specify which of these actions is to be taken when referential integrity is violated. This is true not only in terms of deletion, but also in terms of any insertion or replacement operation. A possible mechanism is to allow the DBA to add a number of FOREIGN KEY specifications to a CREATE TABLE statement. For example:

```
CREATE TABLE shipments
    (supplier_no char (4),
     product_no char (4),
     qty number (3))
    PRIMARY KEY (supplier_no, product_no)
    FOREIGN KEY (supplier_no IDENTIFIES suppliers,
                DELETE OF supplier_no RESTRICTED,
                UPDATE OF suppliers.supplier_no CASCADES)
    FOREIGN KEY (product_no IDENTIFIES PRODUCTS,
                DELETE OF product_no RESTRICTED,
                UPDATE OF products.product_no RESTRICTED);
```

In the case of the shipments table, therefore, the delete operation is restricted to the case where there are no matching shipments for a given product or supplier. This is true also for an attempted update of a product number. In the case of an update on a supplier number, however, the update is carried across to any matching shipments records.

The Knowledge Representation Hypothesis

Both artificial intelligence and database work are governed by a unifying theme which, for lack of a better title, we shall call the knowledge representation hypothesis. That is, in database terms, that:

1. The data in a database should represent something.
2. Whatever is represented is governed by certain rules.
3. The data in the database should adhere to those rules.

This hypothesis can be cast in terms of the problem of database integrity. Database integrity, the application of rules to maintain the logical consistency of a database, is fundamentally a problem of knowledge representation.

Entity and referential integrity are examples of generally applicable integrity rules for relational database systems. A number of other integrity mechanisms may be needed, however, for special applications. This section briefly discusses three such mechanisms that have been proposed in the literature: assertions, triggers and alerters. It also discusses how each mechanism might be implemented in future versions of SQL.

Assertions

Assertions were discussed in the first publications about SQL. An assertion is simply a rule expressed on a database to maintain validity. For example, suppose we define a rule to check that a quantity ordered field always lies within a certain range:

```
CREATE ASSERTION a1
ON sales
DEFINE (qty-ordered BETWEEN 10 and 1000)
```

or consider the following assertion which represents the rule 'every London Supplier must supply product P2'.

```
CREATE ASSERTION a2
ON suppliers
DEFINE FORALL suppliers (IF suppliers.city = 'London')
                        THEN
        EXISTS shipments (shipments.supplier_no =
                        suppliers.supplier_no AND
                        shipments.product_no = 'P2')
```

Triggers

Another sort of integrity constraint is the trigger. A trigger is a more general form of the referential integrity mechanism described above. It is designed to be used mainly to activate a chain of associated updates that will ensure database integrity. Suppose, for instance, our table of suppliers has an extra column which maintains a tally of total shipments for each supplier. The following trigger might be applicable in this case:

```
CREATE TRIGGER T1
ON INSERT OF shipments
UPDATE suppliers
SET Total_shipments = Total_shipments + qty_ordered
WHERE suppliers.supplier_no = shipments.supplier_no
```

Alerters

An alerter is a variant of the trigger mechanism designed primarily to notify users of an important event in the database. For example:

```
CREATE ALERTER R1
ON UPDATE OF sales
    INSERT OF sales
WHERE product_no = 'P20' AND qty_ordered 10000
ALERT beynon
```

The alerter above is designed to notify the stock control manager immediately of any sales order for 10 000 P20s. This might be because such an order would exhaust current stock holdings.

Conclusion

In this chapter we have introduced some initial distinctions between the terms data, information and knowledge, and we have made a rough distinction between a database system which is designed to handle large collections of data, and knowledge base systems which originally were designed to handle large collections of rules. The term knowledge base system is however not well set. Levesque for instance has described a database system as a 'vivid' knowledge base system (Levesque, 1986). By this he means that we can organize certain rule-like knowledge as facts to improve retrieval performance.

Database systems are, however, moving more and more towards incorporating rule-like mechanisms. In this light, we have considered database integrity as a problem of knowledge. Maintaining the integrity of a database is fundamentally an attempt to represent relationships between objects in some limited aspect of the real world. Such relationships define rules about valid states of a database.

Most contemporary database systems offer only primitive mechanisms for implementing such rules of integrity. The majority limit themselves to some implementation of entity integrity through an SQL interface. Referential integrity, and indeed most other forms of integrity, are left to the application systems that interact with the database.

Future versions of SQL look likely to incorporate more explicit mechanisms for the handling of referential integrity. The proposed mechanisms are, however, somewhat untidy in appearance. Integrity rules are strongly typed in terms of their intended use. Little attempt is made to generalize. In the next chapter we begin discussing the bedrock for such generalization in terms of the formalism of production rules.

Problems

1. Which of the following statements are facts and which are rules?
    (a) Paul is married to Gillian.
    (b) For person A to be legally married to person B, persons A and B must be over 16 and of opposing sexes.
    (c) Paul is an employee of the EDS company.
    (d) All employees of EDS think that they should have a good lifestyle.
    (e) Paul does not think he has a good lifestyle.
    (f) Anyone who thinks that he should have a good lifestyle and knows that he does not have a good lifestyle is disappointed.
    (g) In order to determine if someone is disappointed do the following:
        (i)   Find out if he or she works for EDS.
        (ii) Find out if he or she does not think he or she has a good lifestyle.
        (iii) Use the knowledge in (f) above to determine if he or she is disappointed.
2. Take any fragment of program code you have written which validates data for entry to a database. Identify the rules in this fragment.
3. What is database integrity?
4. Entity and referential integrity are said to be inherent integrity

rules of the relational data model. What is meant by the term 'inherent'?

5. Use the PRIMARY KEY and FOREIGN KEY clauses of an SQL create statement to define the EMPLOYEES table in Fig. 2.2.

6. Write an assertion on the database in Fig. 2.3 to stipulate that every project should have a project manager.

7. Assuming each projects record has an employee—total value, write a trigger to update this value when a new record is added to the employees file.

8. Write an alerter to alert the system manager of any changes made to the EMPLOYEES table.

FOUR

Expert Systems

Introduction

In Chapter 2 we provided a brief overview of database systems. In Chapter 3 we started to characterize database systems as limited knowledge base systems. They are limited in the sense that they represent only a subset of what we normally mean by knowledge.

This chapter examines another technology devoted to representing aspects of the real world. In this chapter we identify what is meant by the term 'expert system', and what sort of problems expert systems are designed for. We then consider the distinction between an expert system and an expert system shell, and detail some of the advantages of using shells for expert system development. We devote considerable attention to the architecture of one example shell, demonstrating its syntax and rules of inference. We also consider how the shell explains its behaviour and handles uncertain reasoning.

We conclude by considering a fundamental problem with the present generation of expert systems—their stand-alone nature—and how this is likely to change with increasing proposals for embedding expert systems within conventional information systems.

Expert Systems

There are many definitions available of the term 'expert system'. We shall modify an ordered set of definitions provided by Alex Goodall (1983).

> An expert system is a computer system, that performs functions similar to those normally performed by a human expert.
> An expert system is a computer system that uses a representation of

human expertise in a particular domain in order to perform functions similar to those normally performed by a human expert in that domain.

An expert system is a computer system that operates by applying an inference mechanism to a body of specialist expertise represented in some knowledge representation formalism.

The first definition is drawn in human terms. It captures the fundamental essence of what an expert system involves. Hence, a payroll system would not normally be regarded as an expert system. A human expert does not normally calculate and record the salaries of 20 000 employees. A system which advised personnel managers as to suitable salary increments for given employees, however, would probably fall into the category of an expert system. Experts in human resource management would conventionally be needed for such a task.

The first definition, however, conveys little of the nature of an expert system. How does an expert system work? The second definition moves us closer to this idea. It defines expert systems in terms of mechanisms for representing human expertise. Here we are moving from a human-centred to a more technical-centred definition for expert systems.

This technical direction reaches its conclusion in the third definition. Here, we define an expert system in terms of major technical components: a mechanism to perform inferencing and a mechanism to represent knowledge. It is this latter technical definition which we shall expand upon in this chapter.

History

Expert systems have a comparatively short history (McCorduck, 1978) under the aegis of artificial intelligence or AI. Artificial intelligence gained a name and an area of focus at the Dartmouth Conference in the summer of 1956. The first period of AI research stimulated by this conference was dominated by the belief that a few general problem-solving strategies implemented on a computer could produce expert level performance in a particular domain. As such research developed it was soon realized that such general-purpose mechanisms were too weak to solve most complex problems. In reaction to these limitations, researchers began to concentrate on more narrowly defined problems. By the mid-1970s, a number of expert systems had begun to emerge: DENDRAL, MYCIN, PROSPECTOR, INTERNIST, etc. In 1977, Feigenbaum presented the key insight into the power of the expert systems approach (Feigenbaum, 1977). He maintained that the power of an expert system derives not from the particular formalisms and inference mechanisms it uses, but from the knowledge it possesses. Knowledge, and not problem-solving strategy, is the important thing. It is for this reason that an expert system is often referred to as one example (and a very successful one) of a knowledge base system.

Important Expert Systems

Below we describe briefly some of the most important expert systems in the history of AI.

DENDRAL

DENDRAL and META-DENDRAL were developed by a large research group at Stanford University. Both systems were concerned with various aspects of the elucidation of the structure of compounds in organic chemistry. The project was initiated in 1965 with the specific objective of providing computer support for professional chemists who were not necessarily experts in particular analytical techniques. Moreover, such was its success that it inspired the development of the whole expert systems area (Lindsay *et al.*, 1980).

MACSYMA

MACSYMA is an expert system which was developed at the Massachusetts Institute of Technology for symbolic mathematics. It performs differential and integral calculus symbolically and excels at simplifying symbolic expressions. Designed for use by mathematical researchers and physicists worldwide, it contains hundreds of pieces of knowledge elicited from experts in applied mathematics (Martin and Fateman, 1971).

MYCIN

MYCIN was developed at Stanford University to provide consultative advice on the diagnosis and treatment of infectious diseases. Its knowledge consists of approximately 4000 rules that relate possible conditions to associated conclusions. A panel of experts evaluated MYCIN's performance against medical experts in its particular specialism, and judged its performance at least as good (Shortliffe, 1976).

PROSPECTOR

MYCIN's use of IF–THEN rules stimulated a variety of related systems. PROSPECTOR, a system developed by Stanford Research Institute in association with geological consultants and the US geological survey, was originally developed to help geologists working on problems of hard-rock mineral exploitation. It made headline news in 1982 when it was given the same field study data about a region of Washington State as that given to experts in a mining company. The system concluded that there were deposits of Molybdenum over a wide area. The experts initially disagreed. When exploratory drilling was undertaken however, PROSPECTOR was proved right (Duda and Gaschnig, 1981).

HEARSAY

HEARSAY is a speech-understanding system developed at Carnegie–Mellon University. It was one of the first systems capable of understanding connected discourse from a 1000-word vocabulary. Although this performance is only equivalent to that accomplished by a ten-year-old child, many researchers believe that the ideas incorporated within HEARSAY will play in important role in the future development of expert systems (Erman *et al.*, 1980).

A Typology of Contemporary Expert System Applications

Most contemporary expert system applications fall into a few distinct types (Hayes-Roth *et al.*, 1983):

1. Interpretation systems that infer descriptions from observables. For example, surveillance systems, speech understanding, image analysis, chemical structure elucidation.
2. Prediction systems that infer likely consequences from given situations. For instance, weather forecasting, demographic prediction, traffic prediction, military forecasting.
3. Diagnosis systems that infer system malfunctions from observables. For example, medical, mechanical and software diagnosis.
4. Design systems that develop configurations of objects that satisfy the constraints of a design problem. For instance, digital circuit layout and building design.
5. Planning systems that design actions. For example, automatic programming, robot movement, military strategy.

6. Monitoring systems that compare observations of system behaviour to features that seem crucial to successful plan outcomes. For instance, nuclear power plan monitoring, air traffic control.
7. Debugging systems that prescribe remedies for malfunctions. For example program debugging.
8. Repair systems that develop and execute plans to administer a remedy for some diagnosed problem. For instance, automotive, avionic or computer maintenance.
9. Instruction systems that diagnose and debug student behaviour. For instance, the whole area of computer-aided instruction.
10. Control systems that adaptively govern the overall control of the system. For instance, battle and business management.

Expert System Shells

Most of the early and classic expert systems such as MYCIN were built up incrementally over long periods of time using a traditional AI language such as LISP. As such, the knowledge in such a system was 'hard-wired' as a large chunk of LISP code.

As the knowledge engineering discipline developed it became evident that new expert systems need not be built from scratch in the manner described above, but that they could borrow a great deal from previously built systems. The way to do this was to separate out the domain-specific knowledge in the expert system from that part which drives the system. The former entity is now usually referred to as the knowledge base, while the latter goes under the name of inference engine.

This strategy has resulted in a new category of software tool for knowledge engineering—the expert system shell. A shell is an expert system without the domain-specific knowledge. Here we can make the analogy with a database management system. A DBMS is a tool for building database systems. A shell is a tool for building expert systems. Just as a DBMS is built upon some underlying data model, so an expert system shell is built upon some underlying formalism for knowledge representation.

Advantages of Using Expert System Shells

A number of advantages result from the use of shells. For instance:

1. Rapid prototyping. One of the most difficult phases of expert system development is the construction of the first prototype system. Shells allow developers to rapidly prototype a solution to a problem.

2. Imposed structure. An expert system developed in a traditional programming language such as LISP can be said to be relatively unstructured in the sense that LISP does not impose many constraints on the finalized system. This might be seen as an advantage in that it permits maximum flexibility. It may also, however, be seen as a disadvantage in the sense that it forces developers to resolve problems of detailed structure prior to doing any substantive work. In contrast, shells impose prior structure, thus enabling developers to concentrate on substantive content rather than form.

3. Reducing skill level. A major reason that more expert systems are not available is that there are not enough expert system developers to go around. Shells help to reduce the levels of skill required by developers in effectively supplying some of the required expertise. Thus shells can be a major influence in alleviating the expert system development bottleneck.

Architecture of an Expert System Shell

Figure 4.1 illustrates the architecture of an ideal expert system shell. The shell is made up of a number of components.

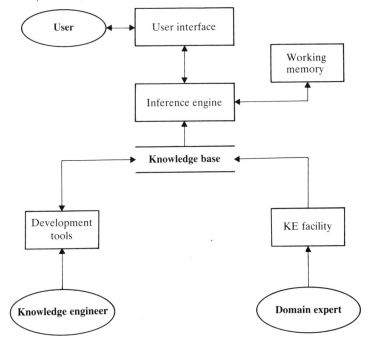

Figure 4.1. Shell architecture

1. The knowledge base. The repository of rules that represent the domain-specific knowledge.
2. The inference engine. That component which drives the system in the sense of making inferences from the knowledge base.
3. The working memory. This is a data area for storing the intermediate or partial results of problem solving.
4. Development tools. These are the means for building and testing the knowledge base. They are designed primarily for use by knowledge engineers.
5. User interface. This mechanism allows end-users to run the expert system and interact with it. One of the most important interactions is with the system's explanation facility. This enables the user to ask questions of the system, about how, for instance, the system came to a particular conclusion.

All shells support at least these five components. Some shells support at least one other component, usually in the form of some knowledge acquisition facility. This is a set of facilities which are designed primarily to enable a domain expert to impart his expertise to the system directly, i.e., without the intervention of a knowledge engineer.

Knowledge Representation

In the field of expert systems, knowledge representation implies some systematic means of encoding what an expert knows about a knowledge domain in an appropriate medium. At a very general level it involves mapping knowledge at the psychological level into a representation of knowledge at the computational level.

Patrick Henry Winston has defined a representation as being 'a set of syntactic and semantic conventions that make it possible to describe things' (Winston, 1984). The syntax of a representation specifies a set of rules for combining symbols and arrangements of symbols to form statements in the representation formalism. The semantics of a representation specify how such statements should be interpreted. That is, how can we derive meaning from them?

Shells are tools for knowledge representation. They allow knowledge engineers to represent the expertise in some domain in a particular formalism. In knowledge engineering, three representation formalisms have found special favour (Nilsson, 1980):

1. Production rules
2. Structured objects
3. Predicate logic.

Of the three, however, production rules are certainly the most prevalent mechanism, particularly in the area of expert system shells and it is for this reason that production rules receive the most detailed attention here.

Rule-based Systems

To give readers a flavour of what is meant by the terms expert system and expert system shell discussed above, let us first detail the characteristics of a typical expert system shell in terms of the characteristics of the knowledge base, and the way in which the inferencing mechanism works with this knowledge base (Jackson, 1986).

Our example expert system shell is designed primarily around the production rule formalism. Production rules are a formalism which has a long history in cognitive psychology and AI (Jackson, 1986). In the expert systems literature production rules are also referred to as 'condition–action' rules, 'situation–action' or 'if–then' rules. Their principal use is in making associations between patterns of presented data and the actions to be performed as the result of such data.

An expert system designed around the production rule formalism is said to be a production system. A production system consists of a rule base, a rule interpreter which decides how and when to apply the rules, and a working memory that holds data, goals or intermediate results. In terms of the architecture for an expert system shell presented in a previous section, the rule base is one example of a knowledge base, and a rule interpreter is clearly what is meant by an inference engine.

The Syntax of Production Rules

Production rules consist of condition and action pairs of the form:

```
IF  condition_1
  AND  condition_2
  AND  . .
  AND  condition_n
THEN  action_1
  AND  action_2
  AND  . .
  AND  action_n
```

which reads, if conditions 1 to n hold, then perform actions 1 through n. Conditions are also referred to as premises, situations or the left-hand side of rules. Actions are referred to as conclusions or the right-hand side of rules.

Conditions and actions are usually made up of 'object–attribute–value' (OAV) triples as in, for instance,

```
paul works production
```

which is to be read as 'paul works for the production department'. A rule incorporating this triple as a condition might be:

```
Rule 1:  IF paul works production
            AND paul employee shop-floor
            THEN paul working-week 40-hrs
```

which is to be read as, 'if paul works for the production department and is a shop-floor employee, then he has a 40-hour working week'.

To make more general rules we need to introduce the concept of a variable. These do not denote particular objects or values, but act as 'place-holders' to which appropriate values can be 'bound'. Such a process of binding is often referred to within AI as 'instantiation'. For example, we can modify rule 1 above to incorporate the variables PERSON and DEPARTMENT:

```
Rule 2:  IF PERSON works DEPARTMENT
            AND PERSON employee shop-floor
            AND DEPARTMENT is production
            THEN PERSON working-week 40-hrs
```

The variable PERSON might now be instantiated with the value 'paul', and the variable DEPARTMENT might be instantiated with the value 'production'.

Working Memory

The most basic function of working memory (WM) is to hold OAV triples. These data are used by the interpreter to 'drive' or 'fire' the rules, in the sense that the presence of these elements in WM triggers some rules in the rule base by satisfying their conditions. For example, suppose we have the following two elements in our working memory:

```
paul works production
paul employee shop-floor
```

These two facts satisfy the conditions in rule 2 above, since on starting the inference process, person will become instantiated with the value 'paul' and department will become instantiated with the value 'production'. This firing will cause the element (paul working-week 40-hours) to be placed in WM.

Backtracking

There may be situations, however, in which the WM contains many elements, some of which will give rise to instantiations which only satisfy some of the conditions. For example, suppose we had the following OAV triples in WM:

```
john works production
john employee foreman
paul works production
paul employee shop-floor
```

In this case, an attempt to satisfy the conditions of rule 2 would mean first that PERSON is instantiated with the value 'john' and DEPART-MENT is instantiated with the value 'production'. Any attempt to match the second condition (person employee shop-floor) against the triple (john employee foreman) will, however, fail. This means that the inference engine must have some means of 'backtracking'. That is, undoing an unproductive move such as the variable bindings above, and exploring alternatives. In our example, this would mean scrubbing the instantiations concerning john and investigating the instantiations concerning paul.

The Behaviour of the Interpreter

The interpreter for a rule base can be described in terms of a cycle of actions:

1. Match the patterns of rules against elements in working memory.
2. If there is more than one rule that could fire, decide which one should fire. This is called 'conflict resolution'.
3. Apply the rule, perhaps adding a new item to WM or deleting an old one. Then go to Step 1.

The data in WM acts therefore both as the means by which rules are fired, and the structure on which the rules act. Usually, a start-up element is inserted into the WM at the beginning of a session to get the cycle going. The session halts if there is a situation in which no rules become active, or if the action of a fired rule contains an explicit command to halt.

In Step 2, the system has a set of pairs consisting of rules and variable bindings or instantiations. In any particular case, however, there may be a number of rules that might fire at the next cycle. For instance, suppose we had the following two rules in our knowledge base:

```
Rule 3:  IF PERSON works DEPARTMENT
            AND PERSON employee shop_floor
            AND DEPARTMENT is production
         THEN PERSON working-week 40-hrs

Rule 4:  IF PERSON works DEPARTMENT
            AND PERSON employee shop_floor
            AND DEPARTMENT is production
         THEN PERSON salary 80_pounds_a_week
```

Further suppose that our working memory consisted of the following two elements:

```
paul works production
paul employee shop-floor
```

Both Rule 3 and Rule 4 can fire with these elements.

Conflict resolution therefore corresponds to the system making up its mind which rule to fire. It is possible to design a rule base such that for all possible configurations of data, only one rule is ever eligible to fire at any one time. Such rule bases are said to be deterministic. That is, you can always determine what rule to fire. Most of the realistic rule bases of interest are, however, nondeterministic. That is, there may be more than one piece of knowledge that applies at any one time. Any rule interpreter must therefore adopt some form of conflict resolution strategy.

The conflict resolution strategy chosen tends to have a marked effect on system behaviour. It should therefore be chosen with care. Good performance from an expert systems point of view depends on sensitivity and stability. Sensitivity means responding quickly to changes in the environment reflected in WM. Stability means showing some kind of continuity in the line of reasoning.

Conflict resolution strategies vary from system to system. There are however four major forms, often used interdependently in any one system.

1. Prioritization of rules. Probably the easiest way of handling rule conflict is to assign some priority factors to rules in the knowledge base. Using this method, if a number of rules are open to firing at any one time, then the rule with the highest priority will be chosen.
2. Rule base recency. Using this approach, a rule should not be allowed to fire more than once on the same data. The obvious way of implementing this is to discard from the set of conflicting rules those instantiations which have been executed before. A weaker version of

this deletes only the instantiations which fired during the last cycle of the interpreter.

3. Working memory recency. For strategy 2 to work, working memory elements must be tagged so that you can tell at which cycle an item of data was added to WM. Another strategy ranks instantiations in terms of the recency of the elements that took part in the problem solving. The rules which use more recent data are preferred to those rules which use data that has been resident in WM for some time.

4. Specificity. Instantiations which are derived from more specific rules, i.e., those rules with a greater number of conditions, are preferred to more general rules with fewer such conditions. Thus, given the choice between the following rules:

    `IF x AND y AND z THEN a`

    or

    `IF x THEN a`

    we would choose the former, because it is more difficult to satisfy and hence takes more current data into account.

Conflict resolution must be handled by any expert system. Some of the strategies discussed above might be handled in any particular expert system by one of two mechanisms. First, they might be incorporated into the inference engine itself. In this sense, they might be called global conflict resolution mechanisms. Second, they might be represented by high-level rules in the knowledge base which direct the inferencing of the expert system. They are local conflict resolution mechanisms. That is, specific to the knowledge base in question.

Backward and Forward Chaining

The inference mechanism described for our example shell is an instance of something called a forward chaining or data-directed mechanism. In this mechanism inference moves forward from data stored in working memory to the goal to be solved. The system does this by attempting to match the facts stored in WM against the conditions or IF parts of the rules in the knowledge base.

Many existing shells, however, employ an alternative inference mechanism known as backward chaining. By this is meant that to run the system, the user normally selects a goal for the system to solve. The system attempts to solve this goal by searching through the knowledge base for a rule which has an identifier in its conclusion, or THEN part, which matches the identifier in the goal. Backward chaining is hence often referred to as goal-directed chaining.

An Example Application

Suppose, for instance, we have built an expert system to handle the process of helping banking personnel to decide whether or not to grant credit to a particular customer. In the knowledge base of this expert system we have the following rules:

```
Rule 1:  IF      customer_status is house_owner
         AND     customer_salary is sufficient
         AND     bank_references are good
         AND     credit_card_references are good
         THEN    credit_rating is good

Rule 2:  IF      net_monthly_salary > (3 * monthly_repayment)
         THEN customer_salary is sufficient

Rule 3:  IF      customer_overdraft is 0
         OR      customer_overdraft < 50
         AND     customer_history is consistently_within_budget
         THEN    bank_references are good

Rule 4:  IF      credit_balance > 50
         AND     interest_charges = 0
         THEN credit_card_references are good
```

Let us further assume that the current goal we wish to run on this knowledge base is to determine the credit_rating for a particular customer. The goal credit_rating is therefore first placed in working memory.

The rule interpreter now attempts to match this goal against the right-hand side of any of the rules in our knowledge base. The only rule that matches is rule 1. Firing this rule means that four further subgoals would be set up for the variables customer_status, customer_salary, bank_references and credit_card_references in working memory.

We now attempt to satisfy the first subgoal in our list: customer_status is house_owner. A value for customer status might be found by asking a question of the user of the form:

```
Is customer a house_owner? (Y/N) _
```

In contrast, the search for a value for customer salary would mean firing rule 2, which places the condition

```
net_monthly_salary > (3 * monthly_repayment)
```

in working memory. Both net—monthly—salary and monthly—repayment would be requested of the user. Assuming that values for these elements are satisfactory, i.e., they set the condition to true, then we will have satisfied the first two subgoals.

Bank—references and credit—card—references are investigated in the same way, by firing rules 3 and 4 respectively. Once these rules are satisfied, processing stops. All the conditions of our top-level rule have now been satisfied. That is:

```
1.  customer_status is house_owner
2.  customer_salary is sufficient
3.  bank_references are good
4.  credit_card_references are good
```

This means that we can write the following conclusion into working memory and display it to the user.

```
credit_rating is good
```

Explanation and Uncertainty

There are two major facets of knowledge which conventional systems have never handled satisfactorily and which knowledge based systems are attempting to handle: the ability to explain reasoning and the capability of handling uncertain or incomplete information. This section is devoted to providing a brief overview of both these subjects, which many people believe to be essential components of the software systems of the future.

Explanation

We begin by discussing an aspect of the interface between user and expert system that is common to most practical expert systems: the ability of such systems to explain their reasoning. It must be said, however, that the explanation facility provided by most contemporary expert system shells is relatively primitive in operation. This is probably a result of the relatively early stage of development of this aspect of expert systems. Indeed, it would probably be true to say that the majority of expert systems provide inadequate support in this area. This is ironic when so many discussions of the value of the expert systems approach revolve around this ability to provide explanations.

Why is Explanation Important?

The ability to explain reasoning is usually considered an important component of any expert system. An explanation facility is useful for a number of reasons (Warner-Hasling, 1983):

1. It can help knowledge engineers debug and test a system during development.
2. It can assure the user that the system's knowledge and reasoning is appropriate.
3. It is useful as a means for instructing the naïve user or some other interested person, such as a student of the area covered by the expert system, about the knowledge in the system.

Inference

At this level, which characterizes the explanation facility available in most contemporary expert system shells, the user may ask very specific questions of the system. The responses to such questions are produced directly from the knowledge base. In other words, the explanation facility examines the knowledge base and performs some relatively simple transformations of the material to produce some reasonable explanations.

   Let us consider the inference process in our credit evaluation system again. The system is started by being given the goal 'What is the credit__rating for this customer?' The system searches for a rule that may satisfy this goal. The most likely choice is rule 1, which causes the system to set itself a number of secondary goals: customer__status, customer__salary, bank__references and credit__card__references. Since the inference engine employed is a backward-chaining mechanism, the system first attempts to satisfy the goal customer__status followed by customer__salary and so on.

   Suppose now on being asked a question such as:

   What is the customer's net monthly salary?

the user wishes to ask why (am I being asked this question)? The kind of response typical of most contemporary systems would be:

```
I am asking about net_monthly_salary to satisfy the rule which states:
if net_monthly_salary  monthly_repayment_multiple
Then customer_salary is sufficient
```

Most contemporary systems allow the user to ask repeated 'whys'. In other words, to track back through a chain of inferences that arrives at a particular state. Hence, a further 'why' asked of our banking example would provide the following dialogue:

```
I am asking about customer_salary to satisfy the rule which states:

If customer_status is house_owner
and customer_salary is sufficient
and bank_references are good
and credit_card_references are good
then credit_rating is good
```

The major problem with this approach is that since the explanation facility can only perform relatively simple transformations of the material in the knowledge-base, the quality of the explanations produced depends to a great extent on how the system is constructed. If the explanations are to be understandable, the system must be written in such a way that its structure is easily understood by anyone familiar with the knowledge domain. Not only this, but the object or variable names used in the system must be suitably mnemonic to represent concepts meaningful to the user.

Facets of Intelligence

The ability to explain one's reasoning is undoubtedly one facet of what we normally understand to be intelligence. In its aim to simulate some aspects of the intelligence of human experts, a knowledge based system must contain some sort of explanation facility. The facility available in the KBS of the moment is undoubtedly crude. Nevertheless, a great deal of research effort is being put into improving this facility, and we will hopefully see some of the practical applications of this endeavour in the relatively short-term future.

Real-life problem solving also demands an acceptance of uncertainty, i.e., the use of fragmentary and uncertain information to reach an estimate of the truth. In their attempt to simulate such problem solving, many expert systems employ mechanisms for drawing inferences from domain knowledge where the facts or rules of inference (or both) are not 100 per cent reliable.

The reasoning employed in such systems is said to be uncertain inference. This means that the facts or inference mechanisms employed cannot effectively determine a given outcome. The question of uncertainty is therefore probabilistic, approximate or 'fuzzy'.

Certainty Factors

One by-product of the MYCIN research effort was a method promulgated by Shortliffe for handling uncertainty using certainty factors. This method was much used in the PROSPECTOR expert system (Shortliffe, 1976).

A certainty factor is the difference between two measures:

$$CF(P{:}E) = MB(P{:}E) - MD(P{:}E)$$

$CF(P{:}E)$ is the certainty of the proposition or hypothesis P given evidence E. $MB(P{:}E)$ is a measure of the belief in P given E, while $MD(P{:}E)$ is a measure of the disbelief in P given E.

Certainty factors (CFs) can range from -1 (completely false) to $+1$ (completely true), with fractional values in between, zero representing ignorance. MBs and MDs on the other hand can range from 0 to 1 only. Thus a certainty factor represents a simple balancing of the evidence for and against a hypothesis.

Shortliffe also provided a formula for updating a certainty factor in the light of new evidence. That is, new information could be combined with previous results in the computation of MBs and MDs. For instance, the updating formula for MDs is as follows:

$$MB(P{:}E1,E2) = MB(P{:}E1) + MB(P{:}E2) * (1 - MB(P{:}E1))$$

This states that the effect of a second piece of evidence $E2$ on the proposition P given the earlier evidence $E1$ is to move the fraction of the distance remaining towards certainty indicated by the strength of the second piece of evidence. The formula has two important properties:

1. It is symmetric in that the order of $E1$ and $E2$ does not matter.
2. It moves MB or MD towards certainty as supporting evidence piles up.

For instance, in the domain of credit assessment we may have two rules giving us two different certainty factors (0.8 and 0.5) for the proposition not to recommend a loan.

```
IF the customer has bad credit_references
THEN do not recommend a loan {CF 0.8}

IF the customer has an overdraft
THEN do not recommend a loan {CF 0.5}.
```

If we apply the updating formula for MBs to these two propositions we get something which looks like:

$$MB(P{:}E1{,}E2) = MB(P{:}E1) + MB(P{:}E2) * (1 - MB(P{:}E1))$$
$$= 0.8 \qquad + (0.5 \qquad * (1 - 0.8))$$
$$= 0.9$$

This agrees with what we would naturally expect to happen when more than one piece of evidence indicates the same course of action. That is, the measure of belief in the hypothesis that a loan should be refused must be increased.

Islands of Computing

Many of the early expert systems such as MYCIN (Shortliffe, 1976), R1 (McDermott, 1980) and PROSPECTOR (Gaschnig, 1982) were originally constructed to solve problems in domains substantially removed from mainstream commercial data processing. One effect of this has been to direct DP professionals to consider and develop applications in their own areas which are heavily inspired by the much publicized work in areas such as medical diagnosis (Reitman, 1984) (Winston, 1984). This has meant that expert system applications in commerce have been seen from a restricted view-point: that of the stand-alone system used for diagnostics, advice or some other popular category emphasized in the historical development of expert systems (Debenham, 1988).

At the present time, expert systems and conventional information systems constitute 'islands' of computing with little or no connection to each other. It is the purpose of this book to portray developments which may act as bridges between these islands (Silverman, 1987). The thesis of this book is that a high proportion of commercial data processing, including all nontrivial database applications, would benefit from the application of expert systems.

Commercial Expert Systems

The whole area of expert systems has, however, been gradually moving out of the academic and scientific arena into the commercial world. For instance, the following list of examples will give the reader some idea of existing applications in this area (Johnston, 1986).

- An expert system which provides exhaustive advice on planning an individual's financial affairs: what to do about investments, insurance, minimizing tax, provision for tax, etc.
- An expert system package for selecting names and addresses for

mailing shots according to who is most likely to respond. Its intended users are mail-order firms who have complex address lists with lots of data on customers' previous purchases as well as demographic information.

- An adviser on the management of company finance. It deals with a large number of issues such as cash flow, return on assets, risks, competition, depreciation, evaluating inventory, and so on. After building up a picture of a company's activities it makes recommendations about future courses to take, such as where to put capital investment.
- An associated adviser on company production intended to reduce lead times and inventories, get around manufacturing bottlenecks and the like.
- An expert system designed to help companies understand and claim for statutory sick pay – a complicated process of getting money back from the state.
- A system designed to help businessmen understand and apply the basics of UK employment law as it relates to the dismissal of employees.

Embedded Expert Systems

Traditionally, expert systems have been built with little or no connection to conventional databases. Hence, their primary mode of working has been to continually prompt the user for the information needed to arrive at a particular conclusion. This we might call stand-alone mode.

Recently, however, research has gone into investigating the important interaction between a rule base and a database. This mode, which we might call database mode, is a major subject of this book.

A rule base need not, however, be totally committed to a database to be useful. Some of the most useful expert systems applications are likely to be embedded in conventional information systems. That is, encased in conventional software which provides inputs to the expert system and receives outputs from the expert system to do further work.

For instance, a stock control system may have embedded within it an expert system module for the reordering of stock. Every time a despatch is made from stock this module is called. The expert system deduces if an order needs to be placed for more stock and for how much. This information is then passed on to a conventional order processing system.

Conclusion

In this chapter we have provided a brief overview of expert systems technology. In a sense, expert systems are the reverse side of database technology. Although databases hold large collections of isolated facts they have no facility for simple deduction. In contrast, traditional stand-alone expert systems store few facts and rely on the user to pass information to the system as and when it needs it to perform certain deductions.

The application of stand-alone expert systems to business, although presently blossoming, is inherently limited. For knowledge engineering to take off as a commercial proposition, the mainstream of conventional data processing departments have to be turned on to the cutting edge of artificial intelligence. This can only be done to a limited extent by the application of stand-alone systems to the fringes of conventional computing. What needs to be done is to employ intelligent software to clean up the exceptions that conventional systems cannot handle. This means embedding knowledge base systems within conventional systems, allowing them to access databases and communicate their results to conventional programs. It is to the range of possible architectures for this wedding of technologies that we turn, in the next chapter.

Problems

1. Describe briefly the differences between a knowledge base system and a database system.
2. What is the difference between a knowledge base system and an expert system?
3. Describe the main architectural components of an expert system.
4. What makes an expert system different from an expert system shell?
5. List three application areas for expert systems.
6. List the major types of knowledge representation employed in AI.
7. Explain the behaviour of a conventional rule interpreter in forward and backward chaining mode.
8. Explain what is meant by the term 'backtracking'.
9. Explain 'conflict resolution'. List three methods of resolving conflict in rule-bases.
10. Why do you think explanation is so important for knowledge base systems?

FIVE

Expert Database Architectures

Introduction

Expert systems research started several years ago with a number of notable academic successes. In recent times, the area has been characterized by a heavy emphasis on commercialization. An expert system is based on two fundamental principles: the appropriate representation of domain knowledge, and the control of this domain knowledge.

Database management systems research has some notable practical successes, particularly in the operational area of database systems. Data models that have been developed for databases share the same overall objectives as knowledge representation schemes for expert systems. That is, to represent some 'slice of reality'.

Clearly, the combination of the two technologies would benefit both expert and database systems. Expert systems, and AI technology in general, will contribute to database systems in areas such as providing a useful reasoning ability in query optimization tasks. DBMS technology will contribute to expert systems in giving them the ability to access large collections of facts and also to apply features such as concurrency control, data security and optimized access to knowledge base items.

There are, however, a number of ways in which these technologies can be combined. It is the purpose of the first section of this chapter to discuss a typology for the available expert database architectures. The second section considers the business needs for such systems. We consider application areas for expert database systems under a number of standard business headings – sales, production, stock control, etc.

Types of Expert Database System

There are a variety of ways in which an expert system might interact with a database. For the purposes of discussion we shall roughly distinguish between four types of expert database system (EDS) (Al-Zobaidie and Grimson, 1987) (Jarke and Vassiliou, 1984a).

1. An enhanced database system.
2. An enhanced expert system.
3. Interdependent expert system and database.
4. A higher-order synthesis. A knowledge base management system.

The first two types are examples of what we might call an evolutionary approach to building expert database systems (Mylopoulos, 1989). This approach treats databases and/or expert systems as starting points and moves in an evolutionary fashion towards the goal of a knowledge base management system. For instance, existing expert system environments such as KEE (Florentin, 1987) would have added to them features such as the efficient use of secondary storage, concurrency control, error recovery and query optimization. This is clearly the most fruitful strategy for research and development within a relatively short-term outlook.

Many other people believe, however, that melding expert systems technology with database technology through some sort of fusion is unlikely to result in a happy marriage. One group maintains that it is far better to employ the known strengths of each tool and allow them to communicate down a common data channel to solve the sort of 'intelligent' tasks required of the new applications. This is the third type of expert database architecture we shall discuss – an interdependent expert system and database (see Fig. 5.1).

Yet another group prefers an alternative, revolutionary, approach to expert database systems. They wish to provide a higher-order synthesis by building a true knowledge base management system (KBMS). We must begin, they say, with a framework for knowledge representation to be supported by a KBMS and then develop a theory of KBMSs based on the features of this framework. They point to the relational data model as an example of the success of this approach. Codd originally proposed a theoretical data model which had to wait a number of years for practical fruition as a relational database management system. In the short term this approach is unlikely to be productive, if only because of the difficulties involved in demonstrating the computational tractability of such schemes. In the long term, however, this approach is probably the correct one, given the likely advances in hardware and software.

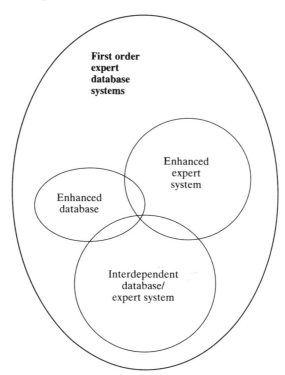

Figure 5.1.   First-order expert database systems

Enhanced Database System

In this type of EDS, a deductive component is joined with a DBMS, thus producing an enhanced database system. Many people, particularly those from the database fraternity, approach AI–DB research as a means for improving DBMSs by dropping 'particles of intelligence' (lots of bright little AI ideas) onto DBMSs. This is the cynical view of enhanced database systems. The enlightened view sees such research as an essential evolutionary step forward towards true KBMSs.

There are three possible ways of linking a deductive component to a DBMS (Jarke and Vassiliou, 1984a).

1. Embedding. Deductive routines are embedded within the DBMS itself, and act as one more facility of the DBMS (see Fig. 5.2).
2. Filtering. User and application program queries are directed through a deductive component before being processed by the DBMS. In this sense, the deductive component acts as an interface between the DBMS and the user or application programs (see Fig. 5.3).

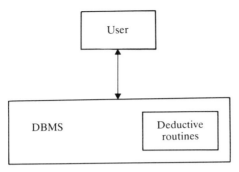

Figure 5.2.   Enhanced database system: embedding

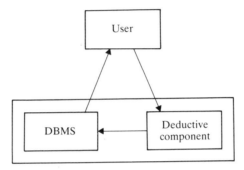

Figure 5.3.   Enhanced database system: filtering

3.   Interaction. The DBMS, rather than user or application programs, interacts with the deductive component (see Fig. 5.4).

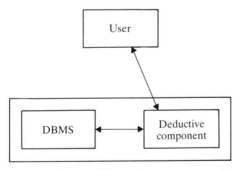

Figure 5.4.   Enhanced database system: interaction

The general idea behind linking a deductive component to a DBMS in one of these three ways is to improve either the efficiency or the functionality of the DBMS. Increased efficiency can result from techniques such as semantic query optimization, which have proved effective for instance in the whole area of relational database systems. Increased functionality can be demonstrated by supporting such elements as natural language interfaces, multiple user views, integrity constraints, and mechanisms for handling incomplete data within the DBMS environment (Stonebraker, 1984b).

Enhanced Expert System

An enhanced database system involves the enhancement of a DBMS with some 'intelligent' software. In contrast, the second type of EDS involves enhancement to an expert system by extending its data management facilities (Jarke and Vassiliou, 1984b). This can be done in one of two ways:

1. Internal enhancement. These are systems which extend the programming language or environment in which the expert system is written (e.g., PROLOG). This in effect gives the expert system its own internal DBMS (Walker, 1984) (see Fig. 5.5).

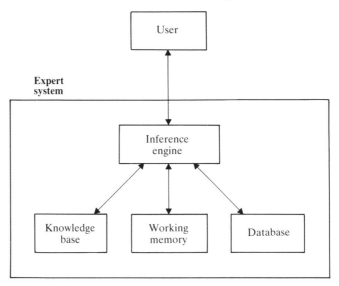

Figure 5.5.   Enhanced expert system: internal enhancement

2. External enhancement. Probably of more interest to commercial data processing is the type of EDS which has been enhanced with external links. That is, the inference engine of the expert system is provided with direct access to a general-purpose, external DBMS. This allows the EDS to be tightly or loosely coupled to the database.
    (a) Loose coupling. In a loosely coupled system there is no dynamic link between the expert system and the database. Data is usually down-loaded to the expert system from the database as

a 'snapshot' prior to the execution of the expert system. When the data in this snapshot has been processed the ES asks the DBMS for new data (see Fig. 5.6).

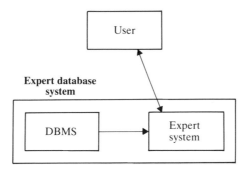

Figure 5.6.   Enhanced expert system: external enhancement, loose coupling

This approach has also been referred to as the compiled approach since it is based on two distinct phases which are repeatedly performed. First, a computation is made on the part of the expert system to generate queries for the DBMS. Second, the DBMS executes the queries and delivers the result to the expert system (Missikoff and Wiederhold, 1986).

One of the major advantages of this approach is of course its ability to use existing databases and thus avoid replicating data unnecessarily. If the expert system is implemented in a logic programming language such as PROLOG, the interface to a relational database appears particularly natural because of the common theoretical foundation of these two tools.

The main disadvantage of this approach lies in the precise separation of the deductive phase and data retrieval phase. If the selected data cannot reside in main memory an additional mechanism must be implemented in order to allow the appropriate paging of data from secondary storage. Finally, an inevitable problem of inconsistency may arise if the data collected from the database is used while the original version of the data is updated.

(b)   Tight coupling. In a tightly coupled system, data is retrieved from the database as and when required during the execution of the expert system. The DBMS, however, still acts in the capacity of a slave to the expert system. This overcomes many of the advantages of the loosely coupled approach, but such free interaction can cause a severe slowing down of expert system performance (see Fig. 5.7).

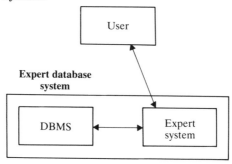

Figure 5.7. Enhanced expert system: external enhancement, tight coupling

Interdependent Expert System and Database

The first two types of EDS involve the enhancement of either the expert system or the database with the facilities available to the other. The third type of EDS we wish to discuss allows the expert system and database to exist as independent systems that communicate down a common data channel. This permits the expert system and DBMS to operate either as two entirely separate systems with their own set of users, or as two cooperating systems. The major problem with this form of EDS revolves around the decision as to where the overall control of system interaction and processing is to reside.

The first possibility is to distribute processing and control such that both systems can operate independently and all interaction is via message passing. Because the two systems are effectively totally independent, however, inevitable problems arise in the areas of data integrity and redundancy (see Fig. 5.8).

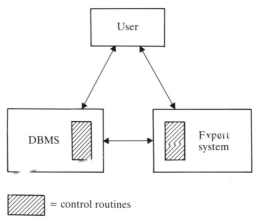

Figure 5.8. Interdependent ES and DB distributed processing and control

A second possibility is to allow either the DBMS or the expert system to dominate. This is likely to be a more flexible architecture, but suffers in its inability to handle the addition of further subsystems satisfactorily (see Fig. 5.9).

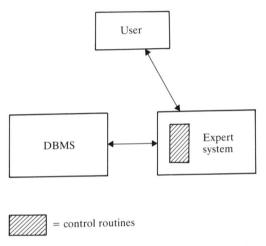

= control routines

Figure 5.9.   Interdependent ES and DB domination of control

Finally, we may envisage a system where processing is distributed, but control resides in an independent subsystem which manages the interaction between database and expert system. A simple example of this approach using a subsystem centred around an object dictionary will be discussed in Chapter 8 (see Fig. 5.10).

Knowledge Base Management System

The approaches described above are all evolutionary approaches to the problem of building a system for managing knowledge. A number of people, however, have suggested that a true knowledge base management system is unlikely to come from a wedding of existing technology. They maintain that a search for a higher-order synthesis is needed. In other words, we need an approach which embraces under one umbrella the facilities of both expert systems and database systems.

A number of initial proposals have been made in this area. From the database side, for instance, the area of semantic data modelling has become increasingly important (see Chapter 9). From the AI side a number of more encompassing knowledge representation formalisms than production rules have been proposed. For instance, object-oriented

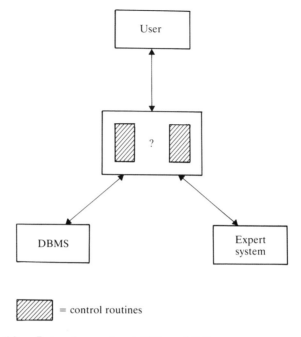

Figure 5.10.   Interdependent ES and DB independent subsystem

systems and first-order logic. These issues will be considered in Chapters 10 and 11 (see Fig. 5.11).

Commercial Applications of Expert Database Systems

Any of the architectures for expert database systems discussed above must prove themselves in the commercial arena. Much so-called new technology has proved a solution looking for a problem, and in many senses a large proportion of EDS work can be cast in this guise. This is fortunately not the whole picture. In this section therefore we move the discussion from architecture to application. We consider the possible application of expert database systems in terms of some of the standard functions of business (Maney and Reid, 1986):

1. Sales and order entry
2. Stock control and warehousing
3. Credit control
4. Management information
5. Business planning
6. Production scheduling

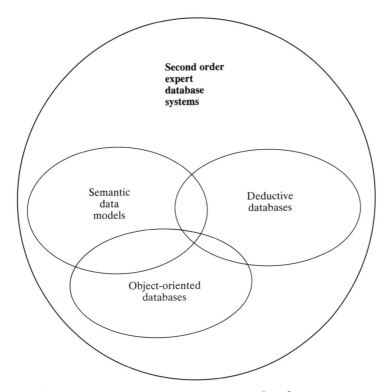

Figure 5.11. Second-order expert database systems

7. Manpower planning
8. Banking.

This of course is not an exhaustive list. But it will serve to demonstrate the important position expert database systems can play in the businesses of the future.

Sales and Order Entry

Orders for products can be prepared in a number of different ways. The most popular is clearly one which involves some interaction between a salesman and a customer. The main objective of the salesman is obviously to maximize revenue. This can be done either by persuading customers to order goods in sufficient quantities or to order goods they would not normally have ordered. An expert database system in this area might be useful in various ways:

1. It would be helpful in continuously analysing previous orders made

by customers, the aim being to build up a profile of customer activity.

2. Such profiles would then be useful in identifying products regularly ordered by the customer which are omitted from the current order but are likely to need replenishment.

3. The customer profile is also of use in identifying products not normally taken by the customer but which are likely to match with his requirements. A reasoned argument may also be produced by the system for the salesman to use.

4. This means that the salesman is likely to improve service levels by better matching products to customers and monitoring the level of customer service provided.

5. The expert database system could serve in a dual role as a sales aid to new customers in the sense that we build up orders through a discussion of customer requirements. One company known to the author sells magnetic media in this manner. The system contains a knowledge base of company products which it uses to match against customer requirements.

Stock Control and Warehousing

A prime area for the application of a deductive system is in the reordering of stock. In conventional information systems this is usually handled by maintaining a reorder level and reorder amount field in the stock record for a product. When a reorder level is reached through successive despatches from stock, the reorder amount is ordered from a supplier.

These fields represent the implicit codification of knowledge. Presumably, the stock control manager arrives at some appropriate figures for reorder level and reorder amount by considering a number of factors. For instance:

1. Size of product. Larger products take up more storage space. Consequently less can be ordered and stored.

2. Turnover of product. A large turnover of products should mean a high reorder level.

3. Value of product. The higher the value of the product the lower the reorder level and amount are likely to be.

4. Bulk buying. The more of a product that can be ordered at one time, the more likely a product is to gain bulk discount.

This method assumes, however, that the delivery periods for reordered stock are known and stable, and also that other factors such as consumption rates are stable. This is unlikely to be true in practice. Suppliers may have different delivery periods for different products. Consumption rates are likely to fluctuate throughout the year and be influenced by the consumption of other associated products.

A better method of systematizing the reordering of stock would be through some form of expert system which continually monitors the ongoing nature of an inventory database. This would have a number of advantages over the conventional two-field approach discussed above:

1. The order value produced by the expert database system is likely to be more accurate than the deterministic value produced by the conventional approach. It is more likely to reflect the ongoing needs of the business.
2. The ordering knowledge in the system is now represented explicitly. It is therefore more amenable to inspection and modification as the rules of the business change.

Associated with the need to order stock is the need to store it. Usually, when stock is delivered to a warehouse its positioning is determined by a combination of information system and warehouseman. The information system will consider parameters, such as the size and weight of items, and suggest a position. The warehouseman will then consider other factors such as the frequency of an item's use and adjust the decision accordingly.

Ideally, when a consignment of items is delivered to a warehouse they should be placed in such a way that the next items to leave the warehouse are easily accessible. The problem comes in predicting which items will leave next. Even the most experienced warehouseman is unlikely to take into account the large number of factors that go into determining the turnaround of individual products. An expert database system, however, can analyse records of previous stock movements to determine the optimal positioning of goods.

Credit Control

Whenever a customer places an order with a company, a decision is made as to whether or not to grant credit. The decision is usually made by comparing the customer's total credit to date against his credit limit. Credit limits are usually set when first effective contact is made with the customer. They may then be revised at periodic intervals, particularly when exceptionally large orders are made.

For business customers the credit limit is usually established through the use of organizations specializing in providing credit information. These organizations do some thorough research on trade references, published accounts and other sources of knowledge about a company. When the customer is an individual a points scoring scheme is frequently used. Points are awarded to customers for being a house owner, for the length of time he has been at his present address, for his salary and so on. The customer's total points score determines the amount of credit which will be extended to the customer.

Credit assessment for both types of customers is a necessarily crude process. For instance, most points systems are extremely crude models of the known relationships between factors and frequently reject potentially fruitful customers. A relatively simple expert system application having say 20 or so rules along the lines of the example in the previous chapter can do far better than most existing points systems, and can be extended to represent far more useful knowledge about customer credit. If such an expert system has links to a database of past customer performance in areas such as quick payment of debts, a customer's credit limit can be a continually changing item.

Management Information

The volume of data which passes through even the simplest company is enormous. A problem faced by every manager is how to interpret such data. How to turn large collections of isolated and hence meaningless facts into information for decision-making.

Conventional management information systems are normally made up of an extensive database providing information in two forms. First, standard reports are produced from the system at regular intervals for the manager's perusal. Second, some form of structured facility such as SQL is provided to enable 'computer-sophisticated' managers to produce *ad hoc* queries on the database. Both such facilities suffer from inherent problems such as being an imperfect means of identifying problem areas, often difficult to use and frequently over-productive in detail.

One of the most successful ways in which AI technology has already infiltrated commerce is by making such reporting functions easier to use. Natural language front ends, for instance, allow 'computer-naïve' managers to express *ad hoc* queries on the corporate database in something approaching everyday English. The manager hence does not need to invest valuable time in learning a formal query language and the physical structure of the corporate database.

Exception reporting is a much used managerial tool. It involves the identification of those areas of the business where actual performance has fallen significantly below or risen significantly above that forecast. Conventional exception reports frequently suffer, however, from providing the wrong level of detail required by the manager. An example of the use of an embedded expert architecture and its usefulness in the MIS domain would be the identification of exceptions. A set of exception-handling 'alerters' could be built into the intelligent database. Such alerters would draw the attention of managers to critical events that have taken place in the organization's data history. The manager could interrogate the system's reasoning or even modify its knowledge for future events.

Business Planning

Planning is fundamentally about preparing for future events. Any planning effort therefore necessarily involves some attempt to forecast factors such as market size, competition, consumption of resources, and so on. Forecasting is usually a process of trying to extrapolate from past and present trends to future trends. Expert database systems are therefore of use in at least two senses. First, as an ongoing means of monitoring company activities and assessing company performance. Second, as a means of taking such indicators and performing some 'expert-like' judgements in terms of probable future patterns.

Mathematical models have of course been much used in this area. The advantage of the expert database approach over conventional practice is its ability to provide more flexibility and ease of use in terms of modelling relationships.

Production Scheduling

The major objective of production scheduing is to optimize the use of the resources of production. Optimization implies balancing a number of subsidiary objectives which are frequently incompatible, e.g. ensuring the satisfaction of customers, maximizing the efficiency of use of scarce resources, minimizing production costs, providing for necessary non-productive activities such as safety and staff training.

Conventional production scheduling systems do not allow for all the subsidiary objectives listed above. Instead, they restrict themselves to producing a feasible programme of work which will use available plant and labour to meet defined quantities for products. An expert system is clearly ideally suited for this sort of problem where a suitable balance is sought between a number of objectives using information that is frequently uncertain.

Manpower Planning

Manpower planning is not an area which brings immediate improvements in a company's profitability. It is, however, an activity which brings significant long-term benefits. Having said this, manpower planning is only really a problem for large organizations. The UK Health Service, for instance, draws up national plans for the recruitment and training of general practitioners.

One fruitful area for the application of expert database systems is in the estimation of staff loss. The estimation of staff wastage by various job categories is normally based around the assumption that staff turnover will remain relatively unchanged over a period of time. This is unrealistic. Staff loss is known to be determined by a number of internal and external factors that can cause rapid changes in staff turnover. External factors include the general state of the economy, competitors drawing upon the same labour pool, and increases in house prices. Internal factors include staff morale. One theory relates staff morale with company size and structure. A company can only grow to a certain size with the same company structure before it starts losing staff.

Both internal and external factors have been extensively studied, at least sufficiently for an expert system to be built to model the known relationships between factors.

Banking

The principal objectives of a high-street bank are to increase its customers, increase the use of its services by customers and to avoid client delinquency. These objectives are normally achieved through utilization of its staff's knowledge of its neighbourhood and clients and their financial situation and needs.

Since knowledge is the fundamental resource of a bank it is not surprising that knowledge base systems have their part to play. For example, take one aspect of a bank's business, namely house insurance. One important contribution a KBS might make would be in identifying likely customers.

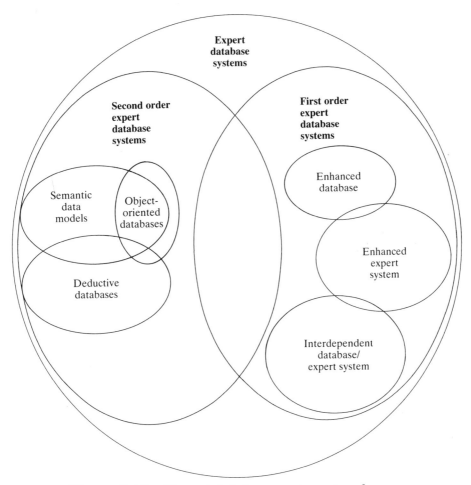

Figure 5.12.   Expert database systems typology

It is usually possible for banking people to identify various classes of customer. One class of home buyers for instance move regularly every three to four years, usually change locality in the process, and generally buy a more expensive home each time. Such customers may be captured in a knowledge base with rules such as: those who have moved regularly are likely to continue the pattern. A collection of such rules run against an existing customer database would identify a useful cross-section of people at which to direct a sales campaign.

Conclusion

In this chapter we have considered a rough typology for expert database systems based upon some evolutionary and revolutionary notions of an appropriate architecture (see Fig. 5.12). We then moved on to give this technical discussion a practical context. We discussed a number of potent applications for expert database systems in industry.

This is really the fulcrum chapter of the book. Chapters to the left of this fulcrum have discussed some of the necessary background material for understanding the concept of an EDS. Chapters to the right of this fulcrum put further flesh on the idea. We first discuss some of the first-order architectures for expert database systems and then move on to provide an overview of a number of different proposals for knowledge base management systems.

Problems

1. Discuss the distinction between an evolutionary and revolutionary approach to knowledge base management.
2. Describe the most credible expert database system architectures for the following applications:
    (a) A system for reordering stock.
    (b) A natural language front-end to a database of management information.
    (c) A system for estimating staff loss.
3. Assess the following application for expert database systems development:

    The UK has some 12 million owner-occupied houses, of which 86 000 were sold in 1986. The vast majority of these sales were financed by mortgages from, in the main, building societies. The standard procedure is that the loan is secured on the mortgaged property such that, if the borrower defaults, the house is forfeit. The building society can then take possession of the property, and sell it to reclaim its loan.

    An accurate valuation, independent of the selling price, is therefore a prerequisite of any loan. The law requires that this valuation is carried out for the building society by a 'competent person'. Usually, this means a chartered surveyor or incorporated valuer.

    The qualified valuer therefore has a captive market. Indeed, mortgage valuations provide a high proportion of the income for valuation practices. At an average fee of seventy pounds per valuation, this market is worth something in the region of sixty million pounds per annum.
4. Could a DBMS imbued with the ability to define entity and refer-

ential integrity be usefully described as an enhanced database system?

5. In what ways do you think a KBMS would need to differ from a DBMS?

6. A decision is structured if the decision-making process can be described in detail before the decision is made. Examples of structured decisions are calculating an employee's tax contribution, pricing normal orders, and so on. A decision is unstructured if the decision-making process cannot be described in detail. This may be because the problem has not arisen before, is characterized by incomplete or uncertain knowledge, or uses non-quantifiable data etc. Examples of unstructured decisions are selecting personnel, estimating bespoke projects, or planning a production schedule (Stow *et al.*, 1988).

    Which type of decision-making is best suited to expert system application?

SIX

Enhanced Database Systems

Introduction

In this chapter we discuss three different examples of the way in which database systems can be enhanced with some form of deductive component. Each example is meant to act as an instance of one of the three types of enhanced database architecture that we discussed in Chapter 5: embedding, filtering and interaction.

We first consider the work done by the POSTGRES team at the University of Berkeley and Delcambre's work on the Relational Production Language as examples of the way in which expert system and data management can be closely coupled in a database architecture. Next we consider a filtering architecture in the guise of a natural language interface. Natural language interfaces are interesting in that many contemporary products are able to snap on to the front of a wide range of database software. Finally we consider the issue of semantic query optimization as an example of the way in which a database management system can interact with a deductive component to improve retrieval performance in particular domains.

The POSTGRES Project

The POSTGRES project at the University of Berkeley, California, is a successor to the INGRES project: one of the first fully developed relational database management systems. Its overall aim is to develop a knowledge base management system by straightforward and natural extensions to the INGRES relational database management systems. Specifically, we examine POSTQUEL, an extension to the QUEL relational query language incorporating rule-like mechanisms (Stonebraker, 1986) (Stonebraker and Rowe, 1987a, b).

Any POSTQUEL command can be turned into a rule by prefixing it with the keyword always, never or once (Stonebraker and Rowe, 1987b). For instance, the following command in POSTQUEL sets the salary of Paul to that of John:

```
REPLACE employees (salary = E.salary)
FROM e IN employees
WHERE e.name = 'Paul'and e.name = 'John'
```

At the time the command is run, this will make the appropriate update to Paul's salary. To turn this command into a more general rule, however, we prefix the command with the term 'always':

```
ALWAYS REPLACE employees (salary = E.salary)
FROM e IN employees
WHERE e.name = 'Paul'and e.name = 'John'
```

The command now appears at least theoretically to be continuously running. In practice, POSTGRES will implement this rule in one of two ways: either by early evaluation or by late evaluation.

Using early evaluation, POSTGRES will awaken this command at the time that John receives a new salary. Hence, the command is awakened whenever a data item which it needs is modified. Using late evaluation, POSTGRES waits until somebody requests the salary of Paul.

Collections of rules can interact in POSTGRES. For example, suppose we have a second rule which sets the salary of David to that of Paul:

```
ALWAYS REPLACE employees (salary = E.salary)
FROM e IN employees
WHERE e.name = 'John'and e.name = 'David'
```

If both rules are evaluated by using early evaluation, then a forward chaining control flow results. When David gets a new salary this is propagated to John, which in turn causes the first rule to fire and propagate the salary to Paul. On the other hand, late evaluation corresponds to backward chaining. A request for Paul's salary will cause a request for John's salary which in turn will cause a request for David's salary.

The crucial question in implementing rules in a conventional relational database system in this manner is clearly one of performance. It is clearly desirable to have some mechanism of determining which rules will fire in the database given a specific command from the user. For instance, suppose the full set of rules for determining salaries in our organization looked as follows:

```
1. ALWAYS REPLACE employees (salary = 10000)
   WHERE employees.age < 35

2. ALWAYS REPLACE employees (salary = 15000)
```

```
WHERE employees.age > = 35
  AND employees.age < = 50
```

```
3. ALWAYS REPLACE employees (salary = 20000)
   WHERE employees.age > 50
```

```
4. ALWAYS REPLACE employees (salary = E.salary)
   FROM e IN employees
   WHERE e.name = 'Paul'and e.name = 'John'
```

```
5. ALWAYS REPLACE employees (salary = E.salary)
   FROM e IN employees
   WHERE e.name = 'John'and e.name = 'David'
```

```
6. ALWAYS REPLACE employees (salary = 17500)
   WHERE employees.name = 'David'
```

Note some fundamental points about rule bases in POSTGRES. The rule base is made up of a number of general rules (1, 2 and 3), a number of rules specifying 'exceptions to the rule' (4, 5 and 6), two of which specify relationships between objects in the database (4 and 5). This makes the rule base fundamentally inconsistent.

Suppose now that the user supplies the following query:

```
retrieve (employees.salary) where employees.name = 'John'
```

Although all six rules can conceivably yield an answer to this query, only two rules will be fired in sequence (6 and 5). Imagine now a rule base of some 1000 rules in which the same order of rules fires. Clearly the key performance measure of queries which exploit rules is to efficiently decide which rule or rules must be fired. Although many rules might apply, few actually apply in practice.

A variety of approaches exist for solving this problem such as theorem proving, the use of flags and indexing (Stonebraker *et al.*, 1986). No concrete conclusions have been reached on the practical validity of either of these approaches, however. The search for an effective mechanism still goes on.

Relational Production Language

POSTQUEL is an extension of an existing formal query language to support rule constructs. In this section we discuss a contrasting approach in which an existing query language, namely SQL, is referenced within a production rule framework. This framework is described as a Relational Production Language (RPL for short) (Delcambre and Etheredge, 1989).

As we discussed in Chapter 4, a conventional expert system is made up of three primary components: a knowledge base, a working memory and an inference engine. Delcambre and Etheredge propose that each of these components be modelled on the formal syntax of the relational data model. Hence, the working memory in RPL is a relational database, the knowledge base is a set of production rules which explicitly exploit SQL statements, the inference engine is a mechanism for directing SQL operation in a forward-chaining manner.

Suppose our working memory in RPL is made up of the following relations:

```
Person (name, mother, father, address)

Childrenof (parentname, childname)

Married (Licence_no, Husband, Wife, Date)

Request (Type, For_whom)
```

A production rule can be expressed on this database to produce a family tree as follows:

```
FAMILY TREE:

FOR ALL
    SELECT *
    FROM Person, Request
    WHERE For_whom = Name
      AND type = 'ancestor'
      AND For_whom ~ = NIL
DO
    DELETE FROM REQUEST:
    INSERT INTO request VALUES ('ancestor', Mother);
    INSERT INTO request VALUES ('ancestor', Father);
    WRITE (Mother ' is the mother of ' Name);
    WRITE (Father ' is the father of ' Name);
END
```

A production rule in RPL is therefore made up of a name, a left-hand side encased in the keywords 'FOR ALL' and 'DO' and a right-hand side encased in the keywords 'DO' and 'END'. The left-hand side of the rule can be made up of any valid SQL query. The right-hand side is made up of a series of file maintenance commands delimited with semicolons: inserts, updates, and deletes.

This architecture for production rules has the following advantages over conventional production rules:

1. The production system can directly access any database that supports an SQL interface.
2. The data structures manipulated by an expert system are explicitly defined in terms of a formal data model.
3. Access to data is formally defined within an expert system via the

query language. This supports manipulation of left-hand side constructs for optimization purposes.

4. The integrity of the data used by an expert system is enhanced by the strong typing available in the DBMS and possibly by an additional mechanism for the enforcement of integrity constraints.

The major problem with this architecture for an expert database system is its likely poor performance. In a conventional expert system, the scratchpad or working memory is held in the computer's main memory. Clearly, for the large databases discussed by Delcambre this is impractical. The production system is therefore likely to be extremely I/O intensive. Having said this, RPL is an elegant solution to the close coupling of data management and expert system.

Active Databases

The POSTGRES work and that proposed by Delcambre may both be considered examples of the concept of an active database (Morgenstern, 1983). A database is active to the extent that it responds intelligently to initiated actions and can itself initiate further actions. Both POSTGRES and RPL can effectively emulate the trigger mechanism described in Chapter 3. An update action which triggers a set of rules under POSTGRES, for instance, can initiate a whole chain of further updates.

Natural Language Interfaces

The normal method of extracting data from databases is via some formal language such as SQL. Many people have, however, criticized such formal languages on a number of fronts. For instance, a user wishing to extract data via a formal query language must construct a query using not only a description of the data, but also a set of syntactical, constructional and navigational elements to encase it. Many of these shortcomings can be overcome by extending or enhancing the user interface in the direction of more informal or 'natural' means of communication. To build such natural language interfaces, however, means investing more 'intelligence' in the interpreter for the language. It is not surprising, therefore, to find that such interfaces have formed a productive area of focus for AI work (Webber, 1986).

This section examines briefly the architecture of a typical natural language interface and considers some of the benefits of this technology for data processing.

The Interface

Most natural language interfaces work by taking statements expressed in English and attempting to construct the closest formal language query which matches this statement. The process of translating statements in some natural language into statements in a formal query language is usually broken down into three stages:

1. lexical analysis
2. syntactic analysis
3. semantic analysis.

Lexical Analysis

Lexical analysis is the process of dividing up a given input sentence into words. For written English, this process is relatively straightforward. It involves a simple algorithm which takes strings of characters delimited by spaces or punctuation to be words.

The list of words that a particular natural language interface can recognize is normally held in a repository known as a lexicon. This lexicon usually represents a small subset of English which directly maps onto elements within a database application such as filenames and attributes and a series of operations that manipulate data in the database. A certain amount of flexibility is normally built into the lexicon. A reasonable range of synonyms for common words, for instance, is normally allowed.

Syntactic Analysis

Statements in a natural language transformed by lexical analysis simply represent flat strings of words. English statements, however, typically represent structured ideas. A first step towards understanding a statement is therefore to assign it some structure. Such an assignment is normally referred to as a syntactic analysis or a parse. Syntactic analysis divides the world of possible inputs into two classes, the legal or grammatical structures, for which a parse can be made, and the illegal, ungrammatical structures, for which a parse cannot be made.

The parsing process must use a set of rules which describe how higher-level structures can be built from lower-level ones. These are so-called rewrite or transformation rules, similar to production rules, as

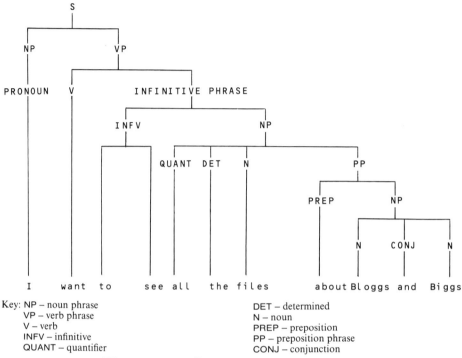

Key: NP – noun phrase   DET – determined
      VP – verb phrase   N – noun
      V – verb   PREP – preposition
      INFV – infinitive   PP – preposition phrase
      QUANT – quantifier   CONJ – conjunction

Figure 6.1. Syntactic analysis of a query

discussed in Chapter 4. For example, one might use rules such as 'a sentence is composed of a noun phrase followed by a verb phrase' (S —> NP VP) or 'a noun phrase contains a sequence of adjectives followed by a noun' (NP —> ADJ* N). A collection of all these transformation rules is referred to as a grammar. Figure 6.1 shows how a common database query expressed in English is parsed as a tree structure.

Semantic Analysis

The final step in the translation process is to assign a meaning to the statement. In other words, we must determine what action the DBMS should take. Actually, semantic analysis is really a combination of two processes that are sometimes viewed separately: semantic processing (determining what a statement means) and pragmatic processing (determining what should be done about it). For instance, consider the following request to a database management system:

'Could you tell me all the managers who are female?'

Taken literally this statement is a request for information about what the system can do. We might reasonably expect a yes or no answer. Actually, what is intended is that the system tells us the names of all female managers.

The techniques used to assign a semantic interpretation to a statement vary widely, usually depending on the way in which other aspects of the NL interface work. We therefore defer this to our discussion of a specific NL interface.

Conducting a Dialogue

Most realistic data processing tasks require more than an understanding of individual statements. For this reason NL interfaces usually include some form of interactive dialogue facility. Consider the following dialogue:

```
1.  User: Who is the manager of the sales department?
    System: Rhiannon Thomas

2.  User: What is her salary?
    System: £20,000

3.  User: Her extension?
    System: 2240
```

This example demonstrates the most important problem with handling dialogues. Individual statements making up a dialogue are often incomplete. To understand these statements the NL system must continually supply a context. It must know, for instance, that the word 'her' in statements 2 and 3 refer to the person named in statement 1.

Semantic Grammars

We now consider the workings of one particular type of NL interface based on the notion of a semantic grammar. The basic idea behind a semantic grammar is that a statement is translated in two steps rather than the three described above. Lexical analysis separates a statement into words. Then these words are analysed for syntax and semantics in a single step.

A semantic grammar, like any other, consists of a series of transformation rules. When a statement is parsed by the grammar it is assigned a structure determined by these rules. The rules are designed so that the structure produced by the parser corresponds closely to that needed by a database query processor. The following example shows a simplified fragment of a semantic grammar used in the Ladder system (Rich, 1984). The colon between symbols stands for 'or'. A ship type, for example, can be a carrier, or a submarine, and so on.

```
S >                QUERY: SHIP-PROPERTY of SHIP
QUERY >            what is: tell me
SHIP-PROPERTY >    the SHIP-PROP: SHIP-PROP
SHIP-PROP >        speed: length: type
SHIP >             the SHIP-NAME: the fastest SHIP2
SHIP-NAME >        Kennedy: Kitty Hawk: Constellation . . . . .
SHIP2 >            COUNTRYS SHIP3: SHIP3
SHIP3 >            SHIPTYPE LOCATION: SHIPTYPE
SHIPTYPE >         carrier: submarine: . . . . .
COUNTRYS >         American: British: Russian: . . . . .
LOCATION >         in the Mediterranean: in the Atlantic: . . . . .
```

Examples of sentences that can be parsed using this grammar are:

```
What is the speed of the Kennedy?
Tell me the speed of the Kennedy.
```

These sentences in fact produce the same parse, even though one is syntactically a question and the other is an imperative statement. Other perfectly good English sentences cannot be parsed, for instance:

```
What is the colour of the Kennedy?
Give me the length of the Kennedy.
```

When a semantic grammar is used, just as when any grammar is used, some parsing technique must be employed to apply the grammar to each input statement. Figure 6.2 shows a parse tree generated from the semantic grammar above.

Since semantic grammars are designed specifically to correspond to the semantics of the target application, it is relatively straightforward to generate a formal database query from a parse tree such as the above. For instance, a procedure might be designed which walks through the tree and performs actions associated with each link (Fig. 6.3).

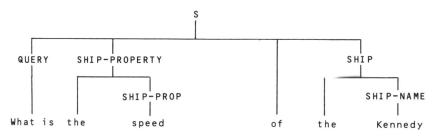

Figure 6.2.   Semantic analysis of a query

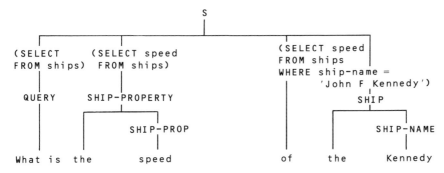

Figure 6.3.   Generating an SQL query

The Pros and Cons of Natural Language Systems

Natural language interfaces have been used effectively as an information centre tool (Harris, 1984). Their most obvious advantage is that people do not have to be trained in the formal syntax of some query language or in the architecture of a particular database. In many senses a natural language interface assumes that all the data relevant to a particular domain is stored in one single or universal relation (Ullman, 1989). This means that for many standard tasks it is probably easier to phrase a natural language query than it is to construct a formal query. Often, the NL statement is considerably shorter than its formal equivalent.

Having said this, NL systems are still not true human-like communication systems. Most existing NL interfaces implement only a restricted version of contemporary English. The systems have very little common-sense understanding and they do not have any realistic world view with which to reason about questions asked of it. When we start to investigate the handling of such concerns the nature of the natural language system changes from one of interface to that of an entire knowledge base system.

Query Optimization as a Problem of Knowledge

Query optimizers are the means by which relational database management systems determine the best way to execute file maintenance and retrieval operations such as selection, insertion, deletion and update. Query optimization is a difficult issue even for the modern range of RDBMS. The complexities grow astronomically when distributed databases are considered (Date, 1986).

This section considers query optimization as a problem suitable for solution by knowledge base systems. It demonstrates, through one simple example, how knowledge base system's work and database system's work are increasingly finding common ground.

The problems faced by a query optimizer can be illustrated using a simple stock database example. The database consists of two tables with the following structures:

```
SALES (product_no, supplier_no, . . .)

SUPPLIERS (supplier_no, supplier_name, . . .)
```

Given these structures, the query 'what are the names of the suppliers of product_no P4?', might be expressed in SQL as:

```
SELECT  DISTINCT supplier_name
FROM    suppliers, sales
WHERE   suppliers.supplier_no = shipments.supplier_no
AND     shipments.product_no = P4
```

There are two basic ways in which this query can be solved.

1. Form a combined record of sales and suppliers information for each record in the sales table. Then extract from the resulting table those records having product_no P4 and display the distinct supplier names.
2. Extract from the sales table those records having product_no P4. Then obtain the correct supplier names from the suppliers table that match with these records.

Let us assume that the database contains 100 supplier records and 10 000 sales records. Further assume that of the 10 000 sales only 50 are for product P4. Using some performance measure such as the number of record I/Os needed to achieve each query implementation, it is clear that the second method is some 200 times more efficient than the first:

1. Read 10 100 records and write $100 \times 10\,000 = 1\,000\,000$ records back to disk. Then read the 1 000 000 records and produce a table in main memory of some 50 records from which the supplier names can be produced. Total $= 10\,100 + 1\,000\,000 + 1\,000\,000 = 2\,010\,100$ I/Os.
2. Read 10 000 records and form a table in main memory of some 50 records. Read 100 records to produce a join of sales information with supplier information. Produce the supplier names from the records in main memory. Total $= 10\,100 + 100 = 10\,200$ I/Os.

This example is sufficient to indicate why optimization is necessary. The question remains, however, of how an optimizer decides on the 'best' strategy for implementing a query. The conventional way of handling this problem in contemporary RDBMS is to treat optimization as a problem of search. Any given query run on the database is first converted into a common low-level representation. A number of plans are then generated for satisfying this query and the cost of satisfying each plan is calculated (Jarke and Koch, 1984).

Clearly, to calculate the cost of each plan, the optimizer must have access to a great deal of statistical information about the current state of the database. For example, how many records there are in each file, how indexes are distributed, and so on. Not only this, the optimizer must usually make reasonable decisions about how much calculation it can reasonably perform without either overloading the system or taking too long to respond to the user. For any given query, there are usually many possible implementation plans. It is therefore desirable for any optimizer to decide upon an appropriate subset from the possibly combinatorially large 'search space' that can result.

It is not surprising, therefore, that query optimizers are being endowed with increasing amounts of artificial intelligence. When data is distributed over a number of sites and machines the number of query-processing possibilities multiplies geometrically. A large amount of 'intelligence' will therefore be needed to meet the optimizing challenges of the distributed databases of the near future.

Semantic Query Optimization

Query optimization is clearly a problem of knowledge. The more 'knowledge' a query optimizer has the more likely it is to come up with an efficient solution.

The conventional approach to query optimization is to use low-level information such as statistics about various processing costs to access individual tables in a relational database. This much researched approach has demonstrated that significant gains in efficiency can be achieved by using such information (Jarke and Koch, 1984).

Over a number of years researchers in the database area have indicated that additional gains in efficiency can be obtained by using higher-level information, particularly information about the semantics of a database. This area of 'semantic query optimization' is the topic of the present section (King, 1981; Hammer and Zdonik, 1980).

An Example Database

Assume we have a global nautical database containing the following tables:

```
SHIPS (Shipname, Shiptype, Deadweight, Owner)

PORTS (Portname, Country, Depth, FacilityType)

CARGOES (Ship, CargoType, Destination, Quantity, Value)

OWNERS (OwnerName, Location, Business)
```

We also maintain a clustering index on the owners attribute of ships file. That is, the ships file is clustered with respect to the owners file. Given a record in the owners file, the corresponding records in the ships file can be accessed much less expensively than a sequential search of ships.

An Example Query

We now wish to express the following query on this database:

> List the destination of cargoes worth less than one million pounds being carried by supertankers over four hundred thousand tons to ports with offshore load/discharge facilities.

This might be expressed in SQL as follows:

```
SELECT  destination
FROM    ships, cargoes, ports
WHERE   deadweight > 400
   AND  shiptype = 'supertanker'
   AND  value < = 1000000
   AND  facilitytype = 'offshore'
```

The conventional approach to query optimization would satisfy this query using something like the following approach:

1. Assume 20 000 records in the ships file, 25 000 records in the cargoes file and 3000 records in the ports file. Read 20 000 ships records and extract those records satisfying the deadweight and shiptype restrictions. Let us suppose we locate 3000 records. We write these back to disk (Total: 23 000 record I/Os).
2. Using the 3000 extracts form a join with the cargoes information by reading 2500 cargoes records a maximum of 3000 times. Write, say, 2000 joined records back to disk (Total: 75 000 000 + 23 000 = 75 023 000 I/Os).
3. Form a further join with ports information by reading the 3000 ports

records and writing, say, 2000 back to disk (Total: $75\,023\,000 + 6\,000\,000 + 2000 = 81\,025\,000$ I/Os).

4. Read the 2000 resulting records and extract the destinations for display (Total: $81\,025\,000 + 2000 =$ a maximum of $81\,027\,000$ I/Os).

Semantic Information

Suppose, however, we had the following semantic information expressed as a series of rules available to our optimizer:

Rule 1: Every ship over 350 tons deadweight can operate only at ports with offshore load/discharge capabilities.

Rule 2: The only ships whose deadweight exceeds 150 thousand tons are supertankers.

Rule 3: Only leasing companies own vessels that exceed 300 thousand tons deadweight.

Rule 1 makes the facilitytype restriction in our query redundant. Indeed we can drop any reference to the ports file entirely. Rule 2 also makes one of the restrictions applying to ships redundant. This allows us to transform the query above into something like:

```
SELECT  destination
FROM    ships, cargoes
WHERE   shiptype = 'supertanker'
   AND  value < = 1000000
```

This transformed query has a cost approaching 75×10 I/Os. Knowing that a clustering index exists on the owners file, which contains only 1000 records, however, makes it fruitful to consider the application of Rule 3. To do this the transformed query would look something like:

```
SELECT  destination
FROM    ships, cargoes
WHERE   value < = 1000000
   AND  ships.owner =
        (SELECT ownername
         FROM owners
         WHERE business = 'leasing')
```

The cost of performing this query would be something in the order of 25×10 I/Os—under a third of our original estimate.

The Value of Semantics

These particular estimates should of course not be taken too literally. They depend on a number of changeable implementation factors such as file sizes, the distribution of indexes and so on. What is important, however, is that the estimates serve to support the contention that semantic query optimization—the incorporation of important domain knowledge into a DBMS—can bring about significant reductions in the cost of processing queries.

Conclusion

This chapter has considered three important examples of enhanced database system as originally defined in Chapter 5. Of the three, natural language interfaces have undoubtedly proved the most successful commercially to date. Semantic query optimizers and embedded rule systems are still largely a research topic at the time of writing. They are unlikely to remain that way, however, for very long. The problems involved in handling large and heterogeneous distributed databases are forcing more and more database vendors to consider dropping particles of intelligence into their optimizers. POSTGRES is only one example of how database vendors are extending their products to make them more well-rounded computer-aided software engineering tools.

Problems

1. Rewrite the production rule below as a POSTQUEL statement.

```
IF PERSON works DEPARTMENT
   AND PERSON employee shop_floor
   AND DEPARTMENT is production
THEN PERSON working_week 40_hrs
   AND PERSON salary 80_pounds_a_week
```

2. What is the RPL statement below attempting to do?

```
FOR ALL
   SELECT *
   FROM customers, loan_details
   WHERE customers.number = loan_details.number
      AND status = 'House_owner'
      AND salary > (3 * monthly_repayment)
      AND bank_references = 'good'
      AND credit_references = 'good'
DO
   INSERT INTO acceptances VALUES (customers.number)
END
```

3. Using the semantic grammar of the LADDER system, indicate which of statements below are parsable:
   (a) What is the Kennedy?

(b)   Give me the speed of the Kitty Hawk.

(c)   Tell me the type of the Constellation.

4.   For what sorts of business area do you think natural language systems are applicable?

5.   What is a query optimizer?

6.   Besides its ability to reduce the cost of processing queries, what other advantages arise from semantic query optimization. Any disadvantages?

SEVEN

Enhanced Expert Systems

Introduction

In this chapter we consider first how the contemporary range of expert system shells handle the problem of database access. We then consider some research proposals for embedding an SQL interface into the architecture of an expert systems shell. Finally, we discuss how the nature of one particular application changes with the various types of enhanced expert systems.

Elementary Data Handling

On the simplest level which is representative of all contemporary expert system shells, the whole population of facts needed by an expert system is represented directly in working memory (Jarke and Vassiliou, 1984b). If the expert system employs a forward chaining inference strategy, then all the data would be requested of the user prior to its execution. If it employs a backward chaining mechanism, the expert system will continually prompt the user on an as-needed basis—that is, as it fires rules in the rule base.

The structure of the data needed by the expert system is therefore defined by the variables as declared in the rule base. This is of course directly analogous to the employment of nonpersistent data in conventional programming.

Internal Data Management

The next step in enhancement is also similar to progression in conventional programming languages such as Pascal. We build into the syntax of the expert system language facilities for handling persistent data (Jarke and Vassiliou, 1984a). At its most primitive this allows rules in the expert system to sequentially access data in an external file, or to sequentially write information to such files.

The LEONARDO expert system shell marketed by Creative Logic, for instance, has built within it a procedural language with most of the syntax of a structured language such as Pascal. As part of this language LEONARDO provides a small set of functions for handling persistent data. LEONARDO can handle three types of files: sequential files, direct access files and files composed of a stream of bytes. For each of these file types LEONARDO provides an open, read, and write function (LEO-NARDO, 1989).

Most vendors of expert system shells however, particularly those based on PCs, have kept the available data management facilities as simple as possible. The argument is probably that additional syntax for external file access is an unnecessary overhead.

More frequently, therefore, we see routines offered for interfacing with stand-alone DBMSs. Such routines build a number of different interface modes characterized by the degree of interaction between expert system and DBMS. We shall discuss three such modes: weak coupling, loose coupling and tightly coupled systems.

Weak Coupling

Weak coupling is probably the most prevalent form of communication between existing expert system shells and DBMS. Fundamentally it involves the ability of the shell to write a formatted file for DBMS input or to read a formatted file produced by the DBMS. On PCs, for instance, many shells permit output of data in Standard Data File (SDF) format intended for import to a Dbase III or IV file. Similarly, Dbase can produce an SDF file for import into the expert system.

Loose Coupling

Weak coupling is communication via an intermediate data file. Loose coupling is direct communication between an expert system and a database. Loose coupling of an expert system with an existing DBMS refers to the presence of a communication channel between the two systems which allows the expert system to extract data from the database prior to inferencing. This implies that only a relatively small subset of data can be downloaded to the expert system at any one time. This is because the data management capabilities of most existing expert system shells are main-memory resident.

Loose coupling is normally achieved by providing some data access commands specific to the shell and to the DBMS. Hence, we may have facilities for opening and closing data files and for reading and writing individual records to and from Dbase IV. We may also have a different set of commands for interfacing with the ORACLE DBMS. Such facilities, however, are usually very primitive. On the retrieval side they frequently amount to little more than a sequential scan of a DBMS file. In this light, a recent paper by Napheys and Herkimer (1989) surveys the loose coupling facilities of three popular implementations of PROLOG (see Chapter 11).

There are a number of reasons why the facilities for expert system/ database integration have been slow to blossom. One reason is that such general links have been low down the priorities list for many developers. Many shell developers can earn a lucrative income from consultancy in the interfacing market. It is often true to say that at least on a mainframe, an expert system is of very little use to a company unless it has links to a company database. Most large organizations using expert systems in a corporate sense have therefore either built their own expert system links to established company DBMSs or employ shell developers to construct such links for them.

With emerging standards in the database market, however, this situation will almost inevitably change. For instance, an alternative approach to the piecemeal one described above is to build an SQL interface within the ES shell (Vassiliou *et al.*, 1983). The main advantage of this approach is that since SQL is becoming the standard interface to most DBMSs, the expert system can be to a certain extent buffered from the need to know much about the idiosyncrasies of the particular DBMS. This includes the need to know about access methods.

The actual implementation of such an interface is still the subject of research. One solution would be to employ a similar technique to that employed with conventional programming languages such as PL/1. That is, embedding SQL statements within the PL/1 code and subjecting this hybrid to a precompiler which sorts out the SQL code from the PL/1 code. When the program is run, the results of a retrieval are placed within appropriately declared program variables. In a similar way an expert system can include a number of SELECT statements within its knowledge base and wait for the results to be deposited back in the expert systems workspace.

The major problem here is one of impedance. SQL operates on

relations or tables rather than individual records. Any SQL select is therefore likely to retrieve more than one matching record that has to be processed by the expert system. The expert system shell must therefore have some means of cycling through a series of instances. In the conventional embedded approach this problem is normally solved by providing the concept of a cursor. A cursor is a pointer to a generated relation. As processing proceeds, this cursor is repositioned within the table. A similar approach is clearly feasible within the expert systems domain.

Tight Coupling

Loose coupling is direct but limited communication between an expert system and a database. Tight coupling is the ideal in which an expert system can interact with a database at any point during its inferencing. This may mean reading records from the database at any point or writing information to the database at any point.

The Level5 shell produced by Information Builders Inc., the developers of the FOCUS 4GL, has some basic tight coupling facilities. Level5 has established mechanisms for accessing a Dbase III database at any point during inference. A rule can embody a looping construct to scan sequentially through a Dbase III file or it can utilize a locate function which moves to the next record whose files match a given pattern.

The logical way of implementing tight coupling, however, to any DBMS is via a general SQL interface as described above. This interface would exploit not only SQL SELECT statements but also file maintenance commands such as UPDATE or DELETE.

An Illustration of Enhanced Expert System Architectures

We shall now consider a commercial expert database system in order to demonstrate how such a system can be implemented in various configurations of expert system and database. The application is from the financial services sector: a personal pension quotation system. First some background.

July 1988 saw British Banks, Building Societies, and Unit Trust Groups being given the right to joint Insurance companies in the personal pension market. The idea was to foster private sector competition in the provision of pension schemes. There are a number of different categories of pension scheme available in Britain. Every one who worked in the UK used to pay a contribution to the state retirement pension scheme (SERPS). As from July 1988, however, people were given the right to opt out from this scheme and pay their contribution into a scheme specific to some company (company pension scheme) or a scheme specifically designed for the individual (personal pension).

The Cymro building society were one of a number of financial institutions who set up a personal pension facility in response to this legislation. The original system at Cymro was primarily a manual system fed initially by one of two forms:

1. Customer information form. This was filled in by a member of staff at one of Cymro's numerous branches as a result of an interview with the customer. It was then posted to head office. A sample customer information form is presented in Fig. 7.1.
2. Pension enquiry form (Fig. 7.2). This was filled in by the customer himself and then posted either to the customer's local branch or to head office. If the customer sent the form to the local branch, it was rerouted to head office.

Once a form was received at head office by a small team of one personal pension expert and two clerical staff, the following steps took place:

1. The branch to be responsible for the customer was determined usually from the customer's postcode.
2. Using the customer information supplied the appropriate pension plan was determined.
3. A detailed quotation was produced for the customer using a piece of applications software previously written for Cymro.
4. A covering letter was produced. If the quotation was a standard case this letter was chosen from a number of standard letters stored on a word processor. A nonstandard case, however, required staff to write a personal letter or to give advice to the local branch manager who responded to the customer.

A number of problems exist in the current system:

1. Computer technology is used to automate a number of functions in the system. The software is however disconnected. Staff have to perform a number of separate steps using different application packages to produce a final response.
2. The expert devotes a great deal of time to determining the appropriate pension plans for customers. This leaves very little time for other important activities such as planning marketing strategy etc.

PERSONAL PENSIONS CUSTOMER INFORMATION FORM

....

BRANCH : .... :

DATE AND TIME OF INTERVIEW : .... :

SIGNED : .... :

DATE SENT TO HEAD OFFICE : .... :

....

Surname and Title : .... :

Forename(s) : .... :

Present Address : .... :

: .... :

Post Code   : .... :

Telephone No.   Home   : .... :   Sex   M/F

Business : .... :

Date of Birth : .... : Marital Status : .... :

Occupation : .... :

Non-Pensionable Income : .... :

Highest Tax Rate : .... : Smoker : .... :

Good Health   Y/N   Existing Pension Arrangements   Y/N

If yes provide brief details of pension type, death in service benefits, likely retirement age/AVCs

Occupational scheme member   Y/N   Contracted Out   Y/N

Preferred Retirement age : .... :

Is the customer looking for a high level of security in their pension?   Y/N

Figure 7.1. Personal pensions customer information form

Take this form into your local branch or post it today to:-

The Cymro Pensions Service, Cymro Building Society, Cymro Tower, P.O. Box 27, Fishermans Wharf, Cardiff, CF41 8PU.

Please send me FREE details on Personal Pensions to suit me.

BLOCK CAPITALS PLEASE

Title : .... :   Name : .... :

Address : .... :

: .... :

: .... :   Post Code : .... :

Daytime Phone No : .... :

Date of Birth : ...... / ...... / ...... :   Sex: M/F

Salary : .... :   Age at which I wish to Retire : .... :

So that we can send the information most suited to your circumstances please tick the appropriate boxes below

Self Employed   : ...... :

Employed – not in a company pension scheme   : ...... :

Employed – in a company pension scheme   : ...... :

Are you currently in the State Earnings Related Pension Scheme?

YES   : ...... :

NO   : ...... :

Any known details of existing pension arrangements

Are you a Cymro account holder?   YES ; ... :   NO . ... :

Name of existing Cymro account

Figure 7.2.   Personal pensions enquiry form

3. When the expert is unavailable due to sickness or attending meetings, the processing of applications has to be temporarily suspended.

After a series of interviews with the expert it soon became apparent that something in the order of 70 per cent of enquiries fell into the category of standard cases. A standard case is one for which the expert could detail with certainty the appropriate outcome given the information provided by the customer. The aim of the proposed expert system was to automate the handling of all the steps involved in producing standard quotations.

The question and answer session shown in Fig. 7.3 represents a condensed transcript of one such interview with the pension expert.

Q. What sort of factors go in to determining a recommendation?

A. Well, the most important factor is probably whether the customer is self-employed or not. If he's self-employed the situation is relatively straightforward. If he's likely to contribute for more than 10 years we'd suggest the Scottish Amicable plan. Under 10 years and we'd offer our own premium account. This is not a pension plan as such but a high interest account of our own.

Q. And what about those not self-employed?

A. Well, this is where it gets a little more complex. Let's consider the exception to the rule first. If somebody is in a company scheme but not in SERPS we probably wouldn't make any recommendation. He's better off as he stands. Somebody in a company scheme and in SERPS however would probably be recommended our premium account.

Q. So what about those people who don't participate in a company scheme?

A. It is at these people that we are really directing our sell. Particularly those in SERPS.

Q. OK, so let's take somebody not in a company scheme but in SERPS. What recommendation would you make?

A. Well, our ideal customer, the person with over 25 years of contributions, would probably be pointed in the direction of the Equitable Union plan.

Q. Ah, so contribution period is important for this type of customer?

A. Yes.

Q. So what about the customer not in a company scheme, in SERPS, and with a contribution period of less than 25 years?

A. Well, to consider the extreme again, those people with less than 10 years contributions would attract our premium account. Those between 10 and 22 years would probably attract a Scottish Widows plan and those between 22 and 25 years would be offered a Scottish Widows or Equitable Union plan depending on the level of security required by the customer.

Q. So what levels of security are we talking about?

A. Those needing high security would be offered Equitable Union. Those needing less security would be offered Scottish Widows.

Figure 7.3. Question and answer session

After some analysis of transcripts like that in Fig. 7.3, it soon became apparent that the following factors are what defined a standard case:

1. The employment status of the customer. That is, whether the customer is employed by some organization or is self-employed.
2. The likely contribution period. This is easily worked out as the number of years to age 65 for men and 60 for women.
3. Whether or not the customer is in a company pension scheme.
4. Whether or not the customer is in the state earnings related pension scheme.
5. Whether the investor wants security from his pension or whether he is willing to take the risk of more venturesome investment for high gain.

Identifying the appropriate interactions between these factors gives us the following rule-base:

```
IF employment_status is self_employed
   AND contribution_period > 10
THEN pension is scottish_amicable

IF employment_status is self_employed
   AND contribution_period < = 10
THEN pension is premium_account

IF employment_status is employed
   AND company_scheme is yes
   AND serps is yes
THEN pension is premium_account

IF employment_status is employed
   AND company_scheme is yes
   AND serps is no
THEN pension is not_recommended

IF employment_status is employed
   AND company_scheme is no
   AND serps is no
THEN pension is check_details

IF employment_status is employed
   AND company_scheme is yes
   AND serps is yes
THEN pension is check_details

IF employment_status is employed
   AND company_scheme is no
   AND serps is yes
   AND contribution_period > = 25
THEN pension is equitable_union

IF employment_status is employed
   AND company_scheme is no
   AND serps is yes
   AND contribution_period < 25
   AND contribution_period > = 22
```

```
   AND security is high
THEN pension is equitable_union

IF employment_status is employed
   AND company_scheme is no
   AND serps is yes
   AND contribution_period < 25
   AND contribution_period > = 22
   AND security is low
THEN pension is scottish_widows

IF employment_status is employed
   AND company_scheme is no
   AND serps is yes
   AND contribution_period < 25
   AND contribution_period > = 22
   AND security is dont know
THEN pension is scottish_widows
   OR pension is equitable_union

IF employment_status is employed
   AND company_scheme is no
   AND serps is yes
   AND contribution_period < 22
   AND contribution_period > = 10
THEN pension is scottish_widows

IF employment_status is employed
   AND company_scheme is no
   AND serps is yes
   AND contribution_period < 10
THEN pension is premium_account
```

Enhanced Personal Pension Systems

Clearly the rule base above can be implemented with some slight modification in most conventional expert system shells. Assuming a backward chaining strategy the user is continually prompted for the data as the rules are fired.

A commercial improvement to this would be to build at the front end a data entry screen which directly emulates the customer information form described above. The operator simply enters this information directly into the system using this screen. An inference module then takes the data entered and fires the appropriate rule in the rule base. This writes an appropriate value for the goal to working memory.

The simplest interaction with a database would involve a write routine that builds up a customer record consisting of the customer's name, address, age, etc. and of course the recommendation. This record is then written to the database file at the end of the expert system run. A standard letter routine can then be periodically run on the customer database to produce personalized letters for return to the branches. The local pensions expert may also periodically run a statistical reporting program which gives him details of how many people have been recommended a Scottish Widows pension.

Weak coupling of the pensions expert to a database can also be implemented in the opposite direction. Rather than requiring the user to enter information off the customer information form or personal enquiry form we assume that the information comes as a file of records to the expert system.

In a weakly coupled system the file of enquiries will be in a format such as SDF amenable to input to the expert system. In a loosely coupled system the file might be a Dbase III file that the expert system accesses prior to inferencing. If we have close coupling primitives then the accessing can be done a record at a time from the DBMS during inferencing.

Conclusion

In this chapter we have considered a number of levels of data management facility used to enhance the expert systems environment. From the internal data management facilities available in most shells, through weak and loosely coupled systems available in some shells, to closely coupled facilities available in very few. The future for enhancement would certainly seem to lie in the direction of a standard SQL interface to DBMS.

Problems

1. Describe the difference between a weakly coupled, loosely coupled and tightly coupled system.
2. Which form of coupling is the most prevalent in contemporary expert system shells?
3. How might SQL be embedded within the production rule language of an expert system shell?
4. Design a table to store details of customers used by the pension expert to select an appropriate pension.

EIGHT

Interdependent Expert and Database Systems

Introduction

In Chapters 6 and 7 we discussed types of EDS which involve the enhancement of either an expert system shell or a database management system with the facilities available to the other. The third type of first-order EDS we wish to discuss allows the expert system and database to exist as independent systems that communicate down a common data channel. This permits the expert system and DBMS to operate either as two entirely separate systems with their own set of users, or as two cooperating systems.

In this chapter we shall use a sample application to illustrate some of the principles underlying a possible architecture for interdependent systems based around a data dictionary (Al-Zobaidie and Grimson, 1987).

An Example Application

We shall assume, for instance, that we are working in the financial sector and have an expert system for assessing whether or not to grant credit to customers. We also have a database of customer information which is maintained on a regular basis. Our expert system can work entirely on its own without any reference to the customers database. Similarly, our customers database can operate entirely independently of the expert system. Usually, however, we would wish to couple our customers database to our credit assessment expert system.

Let us further assume that a subset of the rules in our knowledge base is as follows:

```
IF    customer_status is house_owner
  AND customer_salary is sufficient
  AND bank_references are good
  AND card_references are good
THEN  credit_rating is good

IF    net_monthly_salary > (3 * monthly_repayment)
THEN customer_salary is sufficient

IF  customer_overdraft is 0
  OR  customer_overdraft < 50
  AND  customer_history is consistently_within_budget
THEN bank_references are good

IF   credit_balance > 50
  AND  interest_charges = 0
THEN card_references are good
```

and that one of our files in the customer database looks as follows:

```
CUSTOMERS

CUSTOMER_NO  STATUS        MONTHLY_SALARY  RATING

22456        house_owner    800
22458        house_owner    900
23456        house_owner   1000
24311        house_owner    400
```

The Data Dictionary

The crucial question is, therefore, how can we connect up our database to our knowledge base? The answer lies in the important role of a data dictionary. For each identifier in our knowledge base there will be an associated dictionary item which will link to concrete attributes in our data files (see Fig. 8.1). These dictionary items will then be used by a

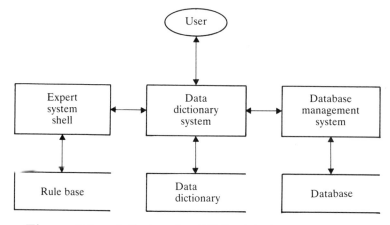

Figure 8.1. A first-order KBS with data dictionary

system which connects attributes in our rule base with values in our database. The data dictionary acts in the capacity of a meta-database of information. A simple data dictionary for the application described above is given below.

```
FILES              OBJECTS

FILENAME TYPE  FILENAME   NAME

credit    k    credit     customer_status
customers d    credit     customer_salary
               credit     bank_references
               credit     card_references
               credit     credit_rating
               credit     net_monthly_salary
               credit     monthly_repayment
               credit     customer_overdraft
               credit     interest_charges
               credit     customer_history
               credit     credit_balance
               customers  customer_no
               customers  status
               customers  monthly_salary
               customers  rating

SYNONYMS

FILE     NAME                 FILE       SYNONYM

credit   customer_status      customers  status
credit   net_monthly_salary   customers  monthly_salary
credit   credit_rating        customers  rating
```

We store information about the files in our system, whether they are knowledge files (K) or data files (D), what information is stored in the data files, what information is used in the knowledge files, and how the data needed by the expert system relates to the data held in database files.

The Data Dictionary System

Sitting atop our expert system and database system we have a data dictionary system (DDS). On entry to the data dictionary system the user will see the following menu:

```
                    DATA DICTIONARY SYSTEM

1.  List Databases
2.  List Expert Systems
3.  Run a Database
4.  Run an Expert System
5.  Access the Data Dictionary

Choose an Option :  _  :
```

Suppose we choose option 4. We wish to run the credit assessment expert system. The DDS will first look to see in the data dictionary if there are any relationships between the proposed expert system and any database files it knows about. Such a relationship does exist between the CREDIT expert system and the CUSTOMERS file. The DDS therefore asks the user whether we wish to run the expert system in stand-alone or coupled mode. If we choose coupled mode, the DDS will ask us the following question:

What is the customer's number?

The DDS knows that customer number is the primary key of the customers table. We would now be expected to enter an appropriate number for the customer we are interested in. Assuming we do this the DDS would then attempt to read a record from the data file having an identifier matching the value entered. If a record is found, all the values for objects in common between the expert system and database system would be set in working memory. In our case, this would be customer_status and net_monthly_salary.

Hence, in the rule below, when the system meets the variable customer_status, a value will exist for this variable in working memory.

```
IF   customer_status is house_owner
   AND customer_salary is sufficient
THEN credit_rating is good
```

If the value is 'house_owner' then the inference mechanism will check the value of customer_salary. This is established by firing another rule in the knowledge base, namely:

```
IF customer_net_monthly_salary > (3 * monthly_repayment)
THEN customer_salary is sufficient
```

We find the value for net_monthly_salary in working memory, and monthly_repayment has been calculated by some other processing in the system. Assuming customer_salary is 'sufficient', another object, namely the goal object credit_rating, will be set with the value 'good'.

Let us further suppose that we want to record this value for credit_rating in the data file. We might do this by using a WRITE comment as follows.

```
IF   customer_status is house_owner
   AND customer_salary is sufficient
THEN credit_rating is good
   AND WRITE credit_rating
```

This addition to our rule will force it to write the value of credit—rating to the customers file if the conditions of the rule are satisfied. To manage this update, the DDS will refer to the data dictionary and find the appropriate attribute in the customers file to update. In our case, this is the rating attribute.

Multi-file Handling

Our example has concentrated on demonstrating how our theoretical interface would handle the interaction between one knowledge file and one data file. This model is easily extended to handling the interaction between multiple interdependent knowledge files making up our knowledge base, and the multiple data files making up our database.

We may, for instance, access a number of data files from any given knowledge file by extending the information held in the data dictionary. For example, we might wish to access another file in our banking database which gives us details of credit cards held by customers. To do this, the data dictionary would need to look as shown in Fig. 8.2.

```
FILES                 OBJECTS

FILENAME  TYPE  FILENAME    NAME

CREDIT      k     credit      customer_status
customers   d     credit      customer_salary
cards       d     credit      bank_references
                  credit      card_references
                  credit      credit_rating
                  credit      net_monthly_salary
                  credit      monthly_repayment
                  credit      customer_overdraft
                  credit      interest_charges
                  credit      customer_history
                  credit      credit_balance
                  customers   customer_no
                  customers   status
                  customers   monthly_salary
                  customers   rating
                  cards       customer_no
                  cards       balance
                  cards       interest

SYNONYMS

FILE1    NAME                    FILE2       SYNONYM

credit   customer_status         customers   status
credit   net_monthly_salary      customers   monthly_salary
credit   credit_rating           customers   rating
cards    customer_no             customers   customer_no
credit   credit_balance          cards       balance
credit   interest_charges        cards       interest
```

Figure 8.2.   The data dictionary

A given knowledge-based system will probably, however, be made up of a number of component knowledge files, organized in some hierarchical manner. Hence, we might have a controlling knowledge file which loads the other knowledge files when appropriate.

```
IF QUERY credit_work
THEN LOAD 'credit'
   AND LOAD 'credit_cards'
     . . .
```

This hierarchical organization would be stored in a number of other tables in the data dictionary.

Multi-record Handling

Above we described how a rule base might interact with a database on a single-record basis. In the relational data model however, most of the data-manipulation facilities are designed around a many-record-at-a-time way of working, rather than the traditional single-record-at-a-time way of working in most procedural languages.

In our system, therefore, it is important for us to have the ability to embed SQL SELECT statements with our knowledge base. Hence, we might decide to use a prior SELECT on our customers file to extract all customers whose customer_status is 'house_owner'.

```
SELECT *
FROM customers
WHERE status = 'house_owner'
```

We would then feed this subset of data through our knowledge base in one clean pass. This is clearly more efficient than requesting the user to continually supply us with identifiers for appropriate customer records. To do this of course we would need some looping mechanism similar to the cursor concept discussed in Chapter 7.

Advantages of the Data Dictionary Approach

There are a number of advantages inherent in the use of a data dictionary system to handle the problem of interdependent expert systems and database systems:

● Flexibility. It enables the user to run expert systems and database systems independently or interdependently.

- Efficiency. It allows expert systems the capability of managing large volumes of data without overloading the expert system.
- Versatility. The data dictionary architecture allows us to add pre-existing expert systems or database systems incrementally.
- Functionality. Expert systems can exploit the data management facilities of the DBMS such as efficient retrieval, concurrency control, and integrity mechanisms.

Conclusion

Data dictionary systems are becoming the glue to connect together various types of software. Data dictionaries, for instance, look like being the major mechanism by which third-party software such as fourth generation languages will be connected to DBMS. Data dictionaries will also offer the means to connect various different databases running under different DBMSs, perhaps even on different hardware. Data dictionaries of the future may even act in the capacity of a store for application-specific logic. Using data dictionaries to handle expert system/database interaction therefore seems to accord with many other developments in computing.

Problems

1. Why is it advantageous to have a system which allows you to run expert systems and database systems independently or inter-dependently?
2. Compare and contrast the concept of a data dictionary as discussed in this Chapter 8 with the idea of a system catalogue as discussed in Chapter 2.
3. Consider how the personal pension system discussed in Chapter 7 would look using an interdependent architecture.
4. What disadvantages do you think arise from using the data dictionary approach?

NINE

Semantic Data Models

Introduction

Data models are central to information systems. Data models provide the conceptual basis for thinking about data-intensive applications. They also provide a formal basis for tools and techniques used in developing information systems.

To reiterate our discussion of Chapter 2, in which we described the relational data model, any data model can be said to be made up of three components (Tsitchizris and Lochovsky, 1982):

1. A collection of data structures for representing objects, attributes and the relationships between objects;
2. A collection of operators for transforming objects;
3. A set of general integrity rules which define valid database states and valid transitions between database states.

Using this approach there can usefully be said to be three generations of data models (Brodie, 1984):

1. Primitive data models. Objects are represented as records grouped in files. Operations provided are primitive read and write operations over records. This covers the facilities available in third-generation languages such as COBOL.
2. Classic data models. The classic data models are the hierarchical, network and relational data models. The hierarchical model is a direct extension of the file model above, while the network model is a superset of the hierarchical approach. The relational model is a significant departure from the hierarchical and network models and has proved influential in recent years.
3. Semantic data models. Despite the important breakthrough of the relational model, the classic data models still maintain a funda-

mental record orientation (McLeod and King, 1980). This means that the meaning of the information in the database is not readily apparent from the structure (schema) of the database itself. Instead, the semantics must be separately specified by the database designer, and consciously applied by the user. The semantic data models attempt to circumvent these problems by using richer and more expressive concepts to capture more meaning than is possible using the classic data models.

It is the purpose of this chapter to give the reader some understanding of what is meant by the term semantic data model (SDM) and what advantages semantic data models have over the relational data model (King and McLeod, 1985).

The Problem of Semantics

The relational data model has undoubtedly provided database practitioners with a modelling methodology independent of physical implementation concerns. Many people, including Codd himself (Codd, 1979), believe however that the relational model does not offer a sufficiently rich set of constructs for modelling the 'real world'. The past decade has therefore seen the emergence of a large range of alternative data models. This collection of data models can be loosely categorized as 'semantic' since their one unifying characteristic is that they attempt to provide more meaningful content than the relational model.

Consider, for instance, the table below:

```
1234    Davies       0000    20000
1342    Jones        1234    16500
2341    Evans        4421    14500
3421    Thomas       2341    12000
3344    Llewellyn    4421    11500
4421    Beynon       1234    15500
```

There are clearly three columns of numbers in the table and one column of names. By organizing this information in a table we assume that the columns are related in some way. The data on its own however conveys very little information—it means little.

In a relational database we assign some rudimentary semantics to the data by associating names with relations and attributes. Thus, for example, we could assign suitable names to our table as follows:

EMPLOYEES

EMP_NO	SURNAME	MANAGER	SALARY
1234	Davies	0000	20000
1342	Jones	1234	16500
2341	Evans	4421	14500
3421	Thomas	2341	12000
3344	Llewellyn	4421	11500
4421	Beynon	1234	15500

The additional information provided by these names together with a certain amount of real-world knowledge would enable most people to interpret this table correctly. In the above example, however, we have deliberately chosen helpful names. This is not a requirement of the relational model. We could have chosen some particularly obscure and remote naming convention for the table and its attributes. There is no inherent need in the relational model for names to accurately reflect real-world concepts (Bowers, 1989). This frequently has the consequence that certain non-facts can be retrieved from a relational database. The database might match a person's name, say Victoria, in one table, to the name of a ship in another table. Imagine the DBMS responding that the sales manager displaces 50 000 tons!

The issue above is, however, somewhat less important than another area of semantics that has received much attention. This concerns the overlap of two concepts such as a manager and employee. In the table above we have treated managers and employees as equivalent to each other. It is quite likely, however, that managers have additional properties which need to be represented. It is at this point that we need mechanisms for handling the principles of abstraction (Peckham and Maryanski, 1988).

The Problem of Abstraction

In other words, the primary problem inherent in modelling any subset of the 'real world' in a computational medium such as a database is the distinction between a human's perception of the 'real world' and the computer's need to organize real-world knowledge into structures for efficient storage and retrieval. A number of researchers have attempted to simplify the design of database systems by providing mechanisms closer to that used by human beings in confronting large amounts of data. This section briefly describes four fundamental abstraction mechanisms that have been found important in such work: generalization, aggregation, classification and association. We translate each mechanism into a formula for relational database design, and then use this material to discuss the richer mechanisms available in one particular SDM.

Generalization

Generalization is the process by which a higher-order object is formed by emphasizing the similarities between a number of lower-level objects. Consequently the differences between these lower-level objects are ignored. For example, an EMPLOYEE object might be considered a generalization of MANAGER, SECRETARY, TECHNICIAN, etc. Generalization is fundamentally the representation of the is_a relationship. We generalize when we say that a MANAGER, for instance, is_an EMPLOYEE (Brachman, 1983).

Generalization can be mapped onto the relational model in a number of ways. For instance, by creating a table for each of the lower-level objects involved in the is_a relationship and a table for the higher-level or generic object. One identifier, such as employee number, is used in all the tables to identify specific instances of both the generic and lower-level objects. We then partition different types of the generic object by values of an attribute common to all the lower-level tables. Job-title would be a good choice in our example. This means that skeleton tables for the generalization hierarchy discussed above might look as follows:

```
Employees(Employee_no, Job_title, ⟨other attributes common to employees . . .⟩)

Managers(Employee_no, ⟨attributes specific to managers⟩)
Secretaries(Employee_no, ⟨attributes specific to secretaries⟩)
Technicians(Employee_no, ⟨other attributes specific to technicians⟩)
```

Aggregation

Aggregation is the process by which a higher-level object is used to group together a number of lower-level objects (Smith and Smith, 1977). In the relational model the higher-level object is usually the relation, and the lower-level objects are regarded as attributes of the relation. For example, ISBN, TITLE, AUTHOR, PUBLISHER and DATE_OF_PUBLICATION might be aggregated together to form a BOOK object. Similarly, NAME, ADDRESS and TEL_NO might be aggregated to form an AUTHOR object:

```
Books(isbn_no, title, author, date_of_publication)
Authors(author_name, address, tel_no)
```

Aggregation is fundamentally a representation of the is_part_of relationship. A TITLE, for instance, is_part_of a BOOK.

Classification

Classification is a form of abstraction in which a number of objects are considered as instances of a higher-level object. Essentially it represents an is_instance_of relationship. For example, a BEST_SELLING_BOOK might be an object which represents all BOOK objects with sales over 10 000.

Classification schemes can be implemented in a number of different ways in relational systems. For instance, one approach would be to utilize the notion of a view using something like SQL. In this way, the classification above might be constructed as follows:

```
CREATE VIEW best_selling_books AS
SELECT *
FROM books
WHERE sales > 10000
```

Another method is to include within the BOOKS table structure an attribute which classifies the sales type of a book.

Association

Association is a form of abstraction in which a relationship between member objects is considered a higher-level set object. The is_member_of relationship embodies the association concept. For instance, the set DATABASE_BOOKS is an association of BOOK objects. Although they look similar, association is fundamentally different from aggregation. Aggregation provides a means for specifying the attributes of a new object. Association is a mechanism for defining an object whose value will be a set of objects of a given type.

Criteria for set membership are usually based on the satisfaction of some condition. For instance, for the DATABASE_BOOKS set the criteria might be TOPIC = DATABASE. This makes association a suitable candidate for the same type of view construction as described in the section on classification.

Limitations of the Relational Model

Although the relational model can be used to model each of the four fundamental abstraction mechanisms described in this chapter, it is still limited in expressive power for representing data semantics.

Most of the formulas for translating a given abstraction into a set of relations are not inherent in the relational data model itself. Even though, for instance, we can simulate the notion of a generalization hierarchy as a series of relations it is left up to the database administrator to construct appropriate mechanisms for exploiting this hierarchy. In other words, the relational model has no direct representation for the concept of 'inheritance'. If a user wishes to see all the information on a particular technician say, the database administrator must have previously implemented some code for joining the generic employees table with the specific technicians table. The notion of inheritance is therefore not inherent in the relational model. It needs to be built as 'icing on the cake'. It is for this reason that a number of more conceptually powerful data models have been proposed.

An Example Semantic Data Model

Most semantic data models are conceptual data models. That is, they are primarily models expressed in abstract or theoretical terms, much in the sense that the original relational data model was expressed. Just like the relational data model, however, a number of semantic data models have achieved a practical realization. We therefore discuss here as an example of a practical implementation of an SDM, the GENERIS system originally developed by a number of researchers at the University of Strathclyde, and now marketed by Deductive Systems Ltd.

GENERIS can be considered as a practical realization and extension of the entity-relationship approach to information modelling as advocated by Peter Chen (1976). In this data model, the real world is modelled in terms of entities (synonymous with objects), relationships and attributes. Entities represent objects in the real world. For instance, an employee and department may be entities important to some organization. Relationships represent named associations between entities. A department employs many employees. Attributes represent the properties that characterize particular entities. Employee number and employee name might characterize an employee; department number and department name might characterize a department.

The only abstraction mechanism directly supplied in the original E–R data model is aggregation. A number of extensions to the model have however been proposed (Teorey *et al.*, 1986). GENERIS takes its inspiration from these so-called extended entity–relationship data models. Hence, one important type of relationship in GENERIS is the class membership or is_a relationship (referred to as a generic association) (Brachman, 1983). Using this relationship one entity can be made a member of another. That is, one entity becomes a class containing the other. For instance, the following facts can be declared in GENERIS as valid commands:

```
Accounts is a department
Manager is an employee
```

Class relationships do not, however, only relate entities to entities. They also may be used to relate entities to attributes and values. Let us assume, for instance, that an employee of an organization is characterized by three defining attributes: name, age and the department the employee works for. In the relational model, the employee entity would be represented by a table, and each of these attributes become column names. In GENERIS, however, each attribute acts as a class for all data-items in the attribute column. Data for Ted Codd, for instance, might be declared to GENERIS in the following way:

```
Ted Codd is an employee
Ted Codd has age 32
Ted Codd has department Accounts
```

This abstraction mechanism has a number of advantages over the relational model. For instance, the relationships between classes and entities fulfil the function of an index in a conventional system. A record can be located directly through any value in any class. This has the effect of maintaining a dynamic index on each column in a table. An employee record can be located by employee name, age and/or department.

Unlike a conventional index, however, a generic association is totally transparent to the user. Indexes do not have to be explicitly built and maintained. They are implicitly built and maintained by GENERIS itself when a table is created and used.

This also enables a significant simplification of queries run on a GENERIS database. Suppose we wished to find the age and department of an employee called Ted Codd. A conventional SQL query for this would look something like:

```
SELECT employee, department, age
FROM employees
WHERE employee = 'Ted Codd'
```

A GENERIS version of the same query would be:

```
DISPLAY department and age for Ted Codd
```

In other words, first, GENERIS does not have to be told that the relevant data is stored in the employees table. It knows that the attributes referred to in the query are stored there. Second, it does not have to be told that Ted Codd is an employee. The generic associations in the data tell it that.

This is fundamentally what we mean when we say that GENERIS is an implementation of a semantic data model. It is a database representation which incorporates more knowledge about meaningful relationships between data.

Rules in GENERIS

As well as a mechanism for supporting factual data, GENERIS also supports production rules. In fact, two types of production rules are available in GENERIS: inference rules and action rules.

Action rules take the form:

$$\langle fact \rangle \quad IF \quad \langle condition \rangle$$

An example of an inference rule would be:

```
manager has status senior IF
  manager manages department AND
  department has budget > 250000
```

Hence, if we expressed the following query in GENERIS:

```
DISPLAY manager status senior
```

the system would use the inference rule above to generate by deduction a list of senior managers.

Action rules have a similar format to inference rules but instead of being used when a query is made, they are triggered by events such as changes in the state of the database. Inference rules do not therefore permanently change the state of the database. Action rules do. In this sense, action rules can be used to implement constraints such as referential integrity (see Chapter 2). For instance, the following rule in association with an action version of the rule above would write the fact 'head office employs Ted Codd' to the database if Ted Codd manages a department with a budget greater than 250 000:

```
head office employs manager IF
   manager has status senior
```

Advantages of Semantic Data Models

As the number of semantic data models has grown, so a number of benefits associated with these types of data model have become clear:

1. Economy of expression. SDMs can represent exactly the same information as the relational model. Much of the information can be extracted, however, with greater ease. Note, for instance, the economy evident in comparing a GENERIS query with a corresponding SQL query.

2. Integrity maintenance. In any data model integrity comes in one of two forms. It is either inherent in the architecture of the model itself, or it can be explicitly programmed via some mechanism. In the relational model most integrity must be enforced explicitly through data validation routines expressed on the database in some such language as SQL (see Chapter 3). SDMs provide a greater range of facilities for the implicit maintenance of database integrity. The entity–relationship model, for instance, provides strong support for a number of inherent constraints. The model inherently supports one-to-one, one-to-many and many-to-many relationships. Insertion and deletion constraints can be defined on such relationships using existence dependencies. If we say that a BOOK entity has a one-to-many relationship with a REVIEW entity, the existence of instances of the REVIEW entity depends upon the existence of an instance of the BOOK entity. Thus, if a BOOK entity is deleted, all REVIEW entries will also disappear from the database (Peckham and Maryanski, 1988).

3. Modelling flexibility. Most traditional data models provide only one mechanism for representing data. SDMs, primarily through their use of abstraction, allow the user to model and view data on many different levels. Through GENERIS's class concept, for example, we can view data on a number of different levels of generalization.

4. Modelling efficiency. Because of their high-level nature, SDMs allow the user a more natural progression from conceptual model to implementation. As we shall discuss in Chapter 12, moving from a conceptual model expressed in something like an entity–relationship diagram to a GENERIS schema is far easier than moving from such a model to a relational schema.

Conclusion

The first research papers on semantic data modelling only started to appear some seven years after Codd's seminal description of the relational model. It could be argued that it is only quite recently that the relational model has achieved a pre-eminence in database terms. It is therefore unlikely that systems based on semantic data modelling ideas will overtake the relational model in the short-term future. Nevertheless, if only because SDMs represent one branch of the convergence of the conceptual modelling work in AI, databases and programming languages, they are likely to have an enormous impact on the information systems of the future (OVUM Report, 1988).

In this chapter we have frequently interchanged the words 'object' and 'entity'. This has served to demonstrate the increasing convergence between the entity–relationship and object-oriented views of the world. Many state-of-the-art products exploit this convergence by referring to themselves as being both object-oriented and adhering to a semantic data model such as the entity–relationship model. This includes GENERIS. There is, however, a clear difference of history between these two approaches. Whereas SDMs are a development of database research, object-oriented systems are much more clearly a development of AI work. Primarily because of this difference of history we consider such systems in the next chapter.

Problems

1. What is a semantic data model?
2. Distinguish aggregation from association.
3. Why is the relational data model limited in its semantic capabilities?
4. What is the following rule in GENERIS attempting to do?

```
supplier has status major IF
   supplier supplies part AND
   part has sales > 30000
```

5. What are the major advantages of SDMs?

TEN

Object-oriented Systems

Introduction

This chapter presents a synthesis between two existing schemes for representing information about the real world. The first of these schemes, namely the relational data model, is from the conventional computing world and has been discussed earlier. The second, namely frame- or object-oriented systems, has achieved some popularity in the field of artificial intelligence.

The author makes the case that frames and relations are similar approaches to the same underlying problem—the problem of representing the objects and relationships present in the real world in a computational medium. The chapter also makes the further point that an object-oriented system may in many ways be considered a higher-order relational model.

It must be noted that the interpretation given here is not the only way of viewing object-oriented systems. Given the fact that there is no clear definition of what constitutes an object-oriented system, however, the clear analogies between frames and relations is a useful organizing principle for a discussion of the field.

Frames

In the mid-1970s, Marvin Minsky, a prominent AI researcher at MIT, introduced a representational mechanism that has become extremely popular in many branches of artificial intelligence (Minsky, 1975). This mechanism Minsky called a frame. A frame is a packet of knowledge which provides a description of some typical object or event. For instance, below we have a frame which defines a salesman object in a personnel domain.

```
Frame: SALESMAN

     AKO: EMPLOYEE
     Name:
     Age:
     Address:
     Salary:
     Start-date:
     Sales-area:
     Sales-quota:
```

This example illustrates the basic elements of a frame.

1. Each frame has a name which identifies the object it describes, e.g. SALESMAN.
2. The frame is made up of a set of descriptions of the object in question termed 'slots', e.g. name, age, etc.
3. Each slot in a frame may be instantiated with a number of different 'fillers'. The only slot instantiated in the frame above is that labelled 'AKO'—short for 'A Kind Of'. This means that the SALESMAN object is a specific subtype of the more encompassing object of an EMPLOYEE.
4. A filler may be either:
    (a) A constant, e.g. Beynon-Davies, Paul,
    or
    (b) The name of another frame in the system, e.g., EMPLOYEE.
5. Slots can also contain so-called 'facets'. Four such facets are used in the frame system which follows (Fig. 10.1):
    (a) The 'unit' facet is a validation mechanism. It specifies that certain information must be given to fill a slot, e.g. unit (surname, forename).
    (b) The 'range' facet specifies the domain of values from which a given filler may be selected, e.g. range (S-Wales, S-West).
    (c) The 'default' facet specifies the value to be taken by the slot, if it is not filled in any other way, e.g. default: emergency.
    (d) The 'compute' facet specifies some procedural attachment. In other words, some piece of logic that will generate a value for the slot, e.g. compute (25 per cent of (gross pay − tax allowance)).

Semantic Nets

Frame systems can be implemented in a number of different ways. One of the most popular is via the notion of a semantic network. In this representation, a frame can be thought of as a complex node in a network, with a special slot filled by the name of the object that the node

```
Frame: SALESMAN

      AKO: EMPLOYEE
      Name: unit(surname, forename)
      Age: unit(years)
      Address: unit(number, street, town, county)
      Salary: SALARY
      Start-date: unit(month, year)
      Sales-area: range(S-Wales, S-West)
      Sales-quota: QUOTA

Frame: S1

      Is-A: SALESMAN
      Name: Beynon-Davies, Paul
      Age: 30
      Address: 38 Nowhere Rd, Llantrisant, Mid-Glam.
      Salary: sal-1
      Start-date: April, 1972
      Sales-area: S-Wales
      Sales-quota: quota-1

Frame: SALARY

      Gross-pay: unit(£.PA)
      Tax-allowance: unit((tax-code) (default: emergency))
      NI: unit(£.PA)
      Net-Pay: compute((25% of (gross-pay – tax-allowance)) – NI)

Frame:  QUOTA

      Product: unit(product-number)
      Number: unit(number-sold)
      End-quota: unit(month, year)
      Commission: unit(percentage)

Frame: SAL-1

      Is-A: SALARY
      Gross-Pay: 10000
      Tax-allowance: 3050
      NI: 1050
      Net-Pay:

Frame: QUOTA-1

      Is-A: QUOTA
      Product: 2468
      Number: 20000
      End-quota: Dec, 88
      Commission: 1%
```

Figure 10.1.   A simple frame system

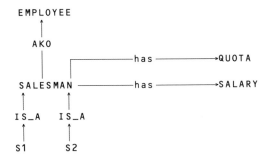

Figure 10.2.   A semantic net for the personnel domain

stands for, and the other slots filled with the values of various properties associated with the object. Figure 10.2 represents a graphic representation of such a network.

Such a system of nodes and arcs is described as being a semantic net because it incorporates some notion of meaning about objects in the real world (Winston, 1984).

Frames may also be considered as systems of hierarchy. In this organization, properties in the higher levels of the frame system are fixed in the sense that they represent things which are typically true about an object. Lower levels in the system have slots that must be filled with actual data.

In this sense, lower levels in the hierarchy are said to 'inherit' the properties that characterize higher levels in the hierarchy. Hence, in our example, S1 being an instance of a salesman, which is in turn a kind of employee, inherits all the properties of an employee of an organization. This is an extremely useful mechanism for reducing the amount of redundant information that needs to be stored in a system.

Relations as Primitive Frames

A relation, as defined in Chapter 2, might be considered as a primitive frame. A relation defines a set of slots or attributes which can be instantiated to provide records. In a relational database system, the system catalogue's relationship to base relations is similar to the notion of inheritance. The system catalogue is organized relationally, and provides a template for each relation in the database. This template details simple validation criteria similar to some of the facets available in a frame system.

Inheritance can also be achieved in a fashion in relational systems through the operation of creating a new table from the join of two existing tables. Hence, for example, a table of employees might be joined with a table of salesmen to detail all the characteristics of employee–salesman.

Frames as Higher-order Relations

In a similar vein, a frame system might be viewed as being a higher-order relational system. Indeed, as we discussed in Chapter 6, many existing relational DBMS vendors such as INGRES seem to be moving towards many of the ideas embodied in frame systems. For instance, the POSTGRES data model includes a procedural attachment facility similar to the compute facet mechanism described above (Stonebraker and Rowe, 1987b).

The relational model was described above as being a primitive frame system in the sense that its notion of inheritance consists of at most two levels: the level of the system catalogue and the level of base relation. In true frame systems the notion of inheritance is multi-level. S1 is an instance of a salesman, a salesman is an instance of an employee, an employee is an instance of a person and so on.

Semantic Modelling

A great deal of material on designing database systems has grown up around the relational model (Howe, 1983). Date has described such material as being examples of semantic modelling (Date, 1986). That is, as being means for modelling the real world in relational terms. Techniques such as entity–relationship diagramming to be discussed in a subsequent chapter are therefore primarily mechanisms for identifying the objects of interest in the real world, and the relationships between such objects. From such diagrams, the objects and relationships are then directly modelled in terms of table structures.

Transforming a semantic model into a relational database, however, involves a substantial loss of real-world knowledge. This is particularly true in the whole area of database integrity. To reiterate our discussion of Chapter 3, integrity is fundamentally about representing the vast range of complex properties of objects and relationships between objects present in a real-world domain. Object-oriented systems allow a closer approximation to this complexity than traditional relational databases.

Consider, for instance, a relational schema in which information about an employee is scattered over a number of different relations. The EMPLOYEE relation contains most of the employee details, the

DEPARTMENT relation contains information on the employee department, the PROJECTS relation contains information about current projects an employee is working on, and so on. As more and more information is stored about employees, the information becomes scattered between more and more relations. Perhaps the primary goal of object-oriented systems is to maintain a direct correspondence between real-world and database objects. In this way objects do not lose their integrity.

As we mentioned in the previous chapter there is considerable disagreement concerning the difference between an object-oriented model and a semantic data model. Roger King has this to say about the issue:

> Semantic models attempt to provide structural abstractions while object-oriented models are geared towards behavioural abstractions. Semantic models grew out of the same sorts of concerns that drove researchers in AI knowledge representation, and object-oriented models were inspired by advances in programming languages. In other words, semantic models are oriented toward the representation of data, while object-oriented languages are concerned with the manipulation of data. (King, 1988)

Object-oriented Development Facilities

Minsky's original ideas for frame systems were cast within the confines of the property list facilities available under the declarative language LISP. Since that time, many experimental knowledge representation languages have been developed, many being frame based. For example, KRL, FLAVOURS, LOOPS, etc. The fundamental characteristic of such languages is the packaging of both data and procedures into structures related by some form of inheritance mechanism.

The term object-oriented, of which frame-based systems are only one form of representation, is used in a number of different disciplines within computing. These include programming languages, databases and AI in general. Object-oriented programming languages developed from SIMULA, an early language developed for simulation work. SIMULA was the first language to introduce the concept of a class or abstract data type—a package of data structures and procedures similar to the frame concept described above. SMALLTALK, a programming environment developed at the Xerox Parc research institute, is, however, probably the best known of the object-oriented programming languages.

Recently, a number of expert system shells have exploited the ideas underlying the object-oriented approach. The LEONARDO expert system shell, for instance, uses a hybrid architecture of frames and production rules with which to build expert systems. Even the developers of conventional database management systems have jumped on the bandwagon. For example, the INGRES team are developing a front end to their relational database which makes explicit use of the frame idea. Applications are envisaged as being built from a system of frames. Frames would be used to get data from the database and display it in a form. Conversely, they would be used to take data from a form and put it into the database. Frames will be allowed to call other frames, and do computations (Durham, 1988).

Object-oriented Database Management Systems

According to a recent report on the future of databases (OVUM Report, 1988), DBMS specifically designed according to some object-oriented model will overtake RDBMSs in the 1990s. The main difference between object-oriented programming languages and databases is that object-oriented database systems require the existence of persistent objects. Objects in an object-oriented programming language exist only during program execution.

The term object-oriented DBMS is used to describe a class of systems with the following capabilities (Ullman, 1988):

1. Ability to define complex objects. That is, the ability to define data types with a nested structure. For instance, a tuple is formed from primitive types such as integers by aggregation, and a relation is built from tuples by set formation. In this sense, an RDBMS can be defined within an OODBMS.

2. Ability to define procedures applying to objects of a particular type and to enforce the requirement that all access to such objects is via these in-built procedures. Thus we might define a stack as a type of object and require that all access to a stack object be via predefined PUSH and POP operations.

3. Ability to distinguish between two objects with the same characteristics. The relational data model does not inherently support this notion of object identity. In other words, we cannot store two identical tuples in a relation since a relation is fundamentally a set and sets do not permit duplicates. In object-oriented systems and indeed in the hierarchical and network data models, however, such a situation is allowed.

Semantic data models focus on the definition of hierarchies of complex objects and on the inheritance of structural components and relationships via mechanisms such as aggregation. Object-oriented models focus on the definition and inheritance of behavioural capabilities, in the form of procedures embedded within types of object (King, 1988).

Commercially oriented DBMSs are still very much a developing arena. At the time of writing, the author knows of at least two: Vbase from Ontologic Inc. (Navathe, 1989) and Gemstone/Opal from Servologic (Ullman, 1989).

Conclusion

This chapter has discussed the synthesis between two presently independent mechanisms for representing knowledge: frames and relations.

A frame is roughly equivalent to a row in a relational database system. A slot is roughly equivalent to the notion of an attribute in a relation. As such, a system of frames is roughly equivalent to a relational database system.

The major differences between frames and relations are as follows:

1. When you create a relation you define its attributes (column names) once and for all. As such, a relation can be said to be deterministic— we know from its structure what should go into the relation, and where to put it. In contrast, a frame is nondeterministic. If we had two frames, for example, each describing a person, the two frames might have completely different slots depending on each of the individual's characteristics. This is the major reason that the slot name is always stored with the slot value in any particular frame.
2. Another difference between a frame and a relation is that in a frame each slot can be associated with a number of different types of information—a data value, facets or procedures. In a relation, at least within existing systems, the attributes have only one type—a data value.

A frame system has all the characteristics of a relational database system without the restrictions of predefined formats and types. It is perhaps for this reason that many RDBMS developers are moving towards many of the concepts involved in the frame-based approach. One report sees databases based on object-oriented models as overtaking the relational model in the commercial world somewhere around the mid-1990s (OVUM Report, 1988). Overall, however, it remains to be seen whether object-oriented databases can demonstrate sufficient performance for handling traditionally large databases. At the moment at least, they seem better suited for non-conventional applications such as, for instance, databases for handling spatial imagery.

Problems

1. Create a simple frame-based system composed of the objects EMPLOYEE, MANAGER, TECHNICIAN and SECRETARY. Explain 'inheritance' in this context.
2. Describe the differences between an object-oriented data model and a semantic data model.
3. Represent the sales database in Fig. 2.7 as a semantic net.
4. What do you think the difference is between an 'a kind of' and an 'is a' link in a semantic net.
5. Compare and contrast relations with frames.
6. Describe the features of an object-oriented DBMS.

ELEVEN

Logic and Databases

Introduction

Ever since Codd brought out his seminal paper on the relational data model researchers have been fascinated with the application of formal logic to databases. This is probably because formal logic has a number of advantages for use in database work:

1. It acts as a rigorous formalism for assessing the informalisms of conventional database work. As such, it has proven a useful vehicle for making explicit some of the hidden assumptions underlying conventional database practice.
2. The same formalism can be used for representing various elements that in conventional database systems require a number of different formalisms. For example:

   (a) defining data
   (b) expressing queries on data
   (c) expressing integrity constraints
   (d) extending conventional databases with deductive facilities.

This chapter acts as a brief introduction to the application of logic in database systems. It is intended to give the reader a flavour of some of the advantages mentioned above. We first provide a brief overview of predicate logic and its application in areas such as the definition of integrity constraints. We then consider a restricted form of logic known as Horn clause form and its use within an automatic theorem prover known as PROLOG. Using PROLOG as our medium we sketch in outline how conventional nondeductive databases are represented and how deductive databases can be represented.

First-order Logic

Logic might be defined as an attempt to ensure reliable human information processing. The problem of ensuring reliable information processing is a very old concern. The earliest attempt to deal with it systematically dates back to the ancient Greeks.

The material of logic is propositions or statements organized in some argument. In order to decide upon the acceptability of some argument it is necessary to make some test. In logic, the main method of doing such a test is to compare the argument of interest against certain abstract patterns. Such patterns are called 'forms'.

Syllogistic to Predicate Logic

Perhaps the most famous of logical arguments is this:

> All men are mortal.
> Socrates is a man.
> Therefore, Socrates is mortal.

This example is usually attributed to Aristotle. It illustrates one of Aristotle's 19 valid forms of reasoning called **syllogisms**.

The key point here is that since these are forms of reasoning, the contents of the statements making up the syllogism are unimportant. It is merely the abstract form of the argument that is important. We may hence recast the above syllogism in more abstract form as:

> All X are Y.
> Z is an X.
> Therefore Z is Y.

If we use a valid form of reasoning, whatever values we give to the variables, it becomes an instance of a valid form. Hence, the syllogism below is a perfectly valid syllogism, even though it might not actually be the case in real life.

> All Welshmen are under six feet tall.
> Paul is a Welshman.
> Therefore Paul is under six feet tall.

Aristotle's 19 valid syllogisms are not, however, able to provide templates for all the kinds of reasoning which we need in everyday life. The next important contribution to formal logic is credited to the nineteenth-century mathematician George Boole.

Briefly, Boole created a means to combine statements together using the logical operators AND, OR, and NOT. Statements of the form, IF A is true AND B is true, cannot be accommodated within the remit of Aristotelian logic. Boole's creation is normally referred to as propositional logic because it deals with such combined statements or propositions.

Gottlob Frege extended Boole's notion of propositional logic to encompass a whole range of new phenomena. Frege's system, which was subsequently developed by many others over the years, is known as first-order predicate logic. It is this branch of formal logic that has been put to the greatest use within modern computing and it is for this reason that we concentrate on predicate logic in this and the following section. The present section provides an informal understanding of the basic building blocks of predicate logic. In the next section we shall introduce a more formal definition of this domain, one which accords more clearly with the database work in this area.

The Basic Building Blocks of Predicate Logic

Let us suppose that we want to represent the following two facts about some organization:

'Watkins manages the sales department'
'Jones works for the sales department'

In predicate logic we represent such facts as:

```
P1:  manages (watkins, sales)
P2:  works_for (jones, sales)
```

Within predicate logic the terms 'manages' and 'works__for' are called **predicates**, while the terms 'watkins', 'jones' and 'sales', are called **arguments**. Predicates and arguments are collected together under the general title of **propositions**, and each proposition may take only one of two possible values, namely, true or false. Hence, each of the following propositions has a **truth value**.

```
P3:  is_a (davies, manager)
P4:  is_a (davies, sales_man)
P5:  is_a (davies, clerk)
```

Each argument in a proposition can be expressed either as a **constant** or as a **variable**. A constant indicates a particular individual or class of individuals. A variable is a place holder in the sense that it indicates that such an individual or class of individuals remains unspecified. Hence, one interpretation of the following proposition might be 'there is some entity X that is a sales_man'.

P6: is_a (*X*, sales_man)

When a variable becomes filled with the name of an object (i.e. a constant), that variable is said to be **instantiated**. We might therefore instantiate X in the proposition above with the value 'paul' to give:

P7: is_a (paul, sales_man)

You will note that in our notation all constants begin with a lower-case letter while all variables begin with an upper-case letter.

There are two other important characteristics of propositions in the predicate calculus. First, the order of the arguments in a proposition must always be fixed in terms of the domain of interest. The user of the notation must therefore decide upon the appropriate interpretative order at the outset, and stick to this interpretation throughout the use of the calculus. Hence if I interpret the following proposition to mean 'paul reports to doug' I cannot later decide to interpret it as 'doug reports to paul'. This would be inconsistent.

P8: reports_to (paul, doug)

Second, a predicate may take any number of arguments. For instance, the statement, 'smith works for sales as a manager' might be represented as:

P9: works_for (smith, sales, manager)

This is said to be a ternary proposition—a proposition with three arguments. Similarly, the sentence 'the company is bankrupt' might be represented by the one-argument or unary proposition:

P10: bankrupt (company)

All the other propositions above are binary propositions—propositions with two arguments.

Logical Connectives

Individual propositions are often referred to as being **atomic**. This means that the internal structure and meaning of such propositions are not determined by the logic. They are in a sense the primitive material from which we build. Such atomic propositions may, however, be combined by the use of **logical connectives**. These include:

AND, OR, NOT and →

Thus we might have the following **compound proposition** which is true for some organization:

```
P11:  works_for (watkins, marketing_division)
      AND manages (watkins, sales)
```

which reads, 'watkins works for the marketing division and manages the sales department'.

The → connective is particularly important in the sense that it allows us to construct rules of the form:

```
P12:  reports_to (smith, jones) → manages (jones, smith)
```

That is, 'if smith reports to jones then this implies that jones manages smith'.

Quantifiers

For predicate logic to handle variables satisfactorily, we need an additional structure called a **quantifier**. Quantifiers are used to indicate how many of a variable's instantiations need to be true for the whole of the proposition to be true. There are two types of quantifier:

1.   The **universal quantifier**, symbolized as ∀.
2.   The **existential quantifier**, symbolized as ∃.

With universal quantification, all instantiations of a variable within some domain of interest must be true for the proposition to be true. With existential quantification, only some of the instantiations need to be true for the proposition to be true. For instance, an example of universal quantification might be:

```
P13:  ∀(X) (sales_man (X)  →  employee (X))
```

which reads, 'for all X, if X is a sales_man, then X is an employee'. In contrast, an example of existential quantification might be:

```
P14:  ∃(X) (manager (X)  →  staff (X))
```

which reads, 'for some X, if X is a manager, then X has staff under him'.

We may also combine these two forms of quantification in any one proposition. For instance:

```
P15:  ∀(X)  ∃(Y)  (employee (X)  →  manager (Y, X))
      every employee has a manager'
P16:  ∃(Y)  ∀(Y)  (employee (X)  →  manager (Y, X))
      there is a person who manages everyone'
```

Constraints

In a database sense, propositions P15 and P16 are actually constraints. This highlights the important role that logic has to play as an unambiguous mechanism for specifying constraints. Consider, for instance, enforcing the classic notion of referential integrity between two sets (relations) of employee data and departmental data. That is, we want to enforce the condition that if a department is disbanded all associated employees are also disbanded. To enforce this constraint in predicate logic would be to write the following statement:

```
P17:  ∀(E)  ∃(D)  (employee (E)  →department (D, E))
```

What we are explicitly saying here is that 'every employee has a department'. What we are implicitly saying is that an employee who does not have a department should not exist in our database.

Logical Inference

In order to process knowledge using predicate logic it is essential that we are able to take some given set of facts and rules, and infer new facts and rules from them. Moreover, we want to do this in a way that we can feel sure of the validity of the results. For example, suppose we have the following facts and rules in our organization:

```
Fact 1:  manages (paul, roger)
Fact 2:  manages (roger, keith)
Fact 3:  manages (keith, william)

Rule 1:  ∀(X, Y)  (manages (X, Y)  →reports_to (Y, X))
Rule 2:  ∀(X, Y, Z)  (manages (X, Y)  AND  reports_to (Z, Y) →reports_to (Z, X))
```

From this knowledge base we can generate the following fact, 'william reports_to roger'. To do this, we first use Rule 1 and Fact 3 to generate the intermediate inference:

```
reports_to (william, keith)
```

We then use this inferred fact with Fact 2 and Rule 2 to infer:

```
reports_to (william, roger)
```

From this description, however, it may appear that the only rules used to generate the desired inferences were Rules 1 and 2 above. In fact, two higher-level rules were used as well, namely:

Modus ponendo ponens (MPP).
$$A \rightarrow B, A \text{ THEREFORE } B$$

'If my program specification is correct then my program is correct. My program specification is correct, therefore my program is correct.'

Universal specialization (US).
$$\forall(X) \ W(X), A \text{ THEREFORE } W(A)$$

'All things which are computers are unreliable. A "simpleton" is a computer, therefore it is unreliable.'

The first rule, *modus ponens*, states that given the truth of proposition A and of the proposition '$A -> B$', we can deduce the truth of B. The rule really follows on from the definition of the $->$ connective. The second rule, universal specialization, simply captures the intuition that if some class of object has a property, then any individual object within that class will have that property.

Such higher-level rules are called **rules of inference**. They are to be contrasted with so-called **domain rules**, such as Rules 1 and 2, whose validity is restricted to the current domain. Rules of inference can be thought of as part of a general control structure within which to manipulate domain rules. When we add such inference rules to the building blocks of predicate logic we turn predicate logic into the predicate calculus. The predicate logic is merely a notation for representing the facts and rules applicable to some domain. The predicate calculus is a mechanism for generating new facts and rules from existing facts and rules. It is a deductive mechanism.

A number of other applicable inference rules within the predicate calculus are given below:

Modus tollendo tonens (MTT).
$$A \rightarrow B, \text{ NOT } B \text{ THEREFORE NOT } A$$

'If my program is correct then it will run. My program does not run, therefore it is not correct.'

Double negation (DN).

$$A \text{ THEREFORE NOT (NOT } A)$$

'My program has run therefore my program has not not run.'

AND Introduction (&int).

$$A,B \text{ THEREFORE } (A \text{ AND } B)$$

'My program has run. My program is correct. Therefore my program has run and is correct.'

Reductio ad absurdum (RAA).

$$A \rightarrow B, A \rightarrow \text{NOT } B$$
$$\text{THEREFORE NOT } A$$

'If my program is correct then it will run. If my program is correct then it will not run. Therefore my program is not correct.'

An Example of Inference

Let us suppose that we have the following rule which states:

```
Rule 3: growing(computer-science) → NOT shortage(computer-science, applicants)
```

'If computer science is a growing subject then there is no shortage of applicants.'
Let us further suppose that we know there is a shortage of computer-science applicants. We can express this in predicate logic as follows:

```
Fact 3: shortage(computer-science, applicants)
```

We now wish to show that this fact and this rule implies that computer science is not a growing subject. We express this as:

$$\text{NOT growing(computer-science)}$$

We can generate an intermediate result by applying double negation to fact 3 above:

$$\text{NOT (NOT (shortage(computer-science, applicants)))}$$

Applying *modus tonens* with our domain rule to this intermediate result gives us the desired inference:

$$\text{NOT growing(computer-science)}$$

PROLOG

In knowledge engineering we are interested in automating the process of generating a set of inferences, to prove the validity of a particular conclusion. There are a number of fundamental difficulties in applying predicate calculus to this task. For instance, in predicate logic there is no mechanism for deciding upon which rule of inference or domain rule to apply next. It is not clear from a completed proof how we decided on which rules to apply, and in which particular order.

All statements in predicate logic can however be expressed in a simple representation known as clause form. When statements are expressed in clause form only one rule of inference need be applied to draw conclusions, instead of a number of rules applied to a number of different statements.

An especially convenient clause form is known as Horn clause form after its inventor Alfred Horn. Since we need only one rule of inference to apply to Horn clauses, it becomes feasible to write a piece of software to continually apply this rule. Hence we have the PROLOG interpreter.

The rule of interest is known as Robinson's resolution principle, in honour of the mathematician and computer scientist J. A. Robinson who discovered it. This single rule for drawing inferences led to the development of an algorithm which could be implemented as a piece of software. The most successful piece of such software is undoubtedly PROLOG.

PROLOG, which stands for PROgramming in LOGic, is now a well-established programming language, particularly since its adoption as one of the central mechanisms in Japan's fifth-generation project. Programs expressed in logic can be viewed as an extension of the relational data model discussed earlier. They allow us to express not only the facts making up our database, but also rules by which we can generate new facts. Those readers interested in PROLOG and logic programming in general are referred to Bharath (1986), Clocksin and Mellish (1981), Walker (1984), Kowalski (1985), Gallaire and Minker (1978).

Logic and Relational Databases

Let us assume we are given the problem of building up a database of sales information for a company over a period of time. We initially build up information on annual sales by customer in the following way. We input facts into a PROLOG database by means of two commands, 'asserta' and 'assertz'. 'Asserta' will insert a fact at the beginning of the database; 'assertz' will append a fact to the end of the database. For example:

```
?- asserta(sales_to(macdonald, 10000)).
?- assertz(sales_to(jones, 5000)).
```

The characters '?-' represent the prompt of the PROLOG interpreter. To see all the facts in the database we type the command:

```
?- listall.
```

and the system replies:

```
sales_to(macdonald, 10000).
sales_to(jones, 5000).
sales_to(macgregor, 7000).
sales_to(smith, 15000).
```

These are the facts or assertions expressed about the sales database. Each fact is made up of a 'predicate'—sales_to—and a number of constants—macdonald, 10000. PROLOG also has facilities for the main-tenance of its database. For instance, to remove a fact from the database we can use the command retract:

```
?- retract(sales_to(smith, 15000)).
```

The normal way of querying a PROLOG database is to type in a fact with variables in appropriate places. For instance, suppose we wanted to extract all the sales for Macgregor. We might use the following query:

```
?- sales_to(macgregor, Sales).
```

and the system would reply:

```
Sales = 7000
```

Note that PROLOG recognizes the differences between literal values such as macgregor and variables such as Sales by the appropriate use of capitals.

A major benefit claimed for logic-based systems is that they are readily extensible. That is, PROLOG systems can grow with company requirements, as circumstances change. For instance, let us suppose that at some later date our company requirements change. It is decided now that we wish to analyse sales by geographical area. To do this, we add the following information to our database:

```
based(macdonald, scotland).
based(macgregor, scotland).
based(jones, wales).
based(smith, england).
```

If we now wish to produce a breakdown of sales by country, we might use the following query:

```
?- based(Name, scotland), sales_to(Name, Sales).
```

The comma stands for the logical connective AND.

PROLOG at work

When we ask a question of the database which consists of two or more goals separated by commas (or ANDs) in this way, the PROLOG interpreter does the following:

1. It tries first to satisfy the leftmost goal.
2. It starts the search at the top of the list of facts which have the required predicate. In this case, 'based'.
3. It is able to satisfy the first goal by instantiating the variable Name to the value macdonald.
4. Then it tries to satisfy the goal to the right. In this case, the goal:

    ```
    sales_to(Name, Sales).
    ```

5. The second goal looks as if it has two variables: Name and Sales. In fact, it only has one, because Name has already been instantiated with the value macdonald. PROLOG therefore treats the second goal as if it is:

    ```
    sales_to(macdonald, Sales)
    ```

6. The PROLOG interpreter searches from the top of the facts with the predicate 'sales_to' in an attempt to satisfy this second goal. It does so by matching with the fact:

    ```
    sales_to(macdonald, 10000)
    ```

    and instantiating the variable Sales with value 10 000.
7. Both the goals have been satisfied, so it prints out the solution:

    ```
    Name = macdonald
    Sales = 7000
    ```

8. PROLOG will, however, not stop there. It will prompt the user to continue the search. This means that it will first search the sales_to facts for another clause for macdonald.

9. Finding none, it will then try to satisfy the first goal again from the point it left off. That is, it will search for another customer resident in Scotland, but will ignore the first fact already examined.
10. It finds another Scottish customer and proceeds to satisfy the second goal by searching from the top of the sales_to facts again. By the same process as above, it will eventually instantiate the variables with the values:

```
Name = macgregor
Sales = 7000
```

All this should sound familiar in the sense that the process of satisfying multiple goals in this manner is really another instance of 'backtracking' (see Chapter 4). We could clearly express a multiple query of this nature for each of the countries in the database. If, however, the query is one we need to regularly run on the database, it would be far easier simply to include the following rule:

```
breakdown_country(Country, Sales) :-
    based(Customer, Country),
    sales_to(Customer, Sales).
```

Rules are made up of a mixture of predicates, constants, variables (Country, Sales, etc.) and logical connectives. ':-' represents the 'implies' connective.

At yet a further stage, a requirement emerges to break down the information by area manager. We therefore add the following information:

```
area_manager(bloggs, england).
area_manager(bloggs, wales).
area_manager(macrae, scotland).
```

and the following rule:

```
breakdown_manager(Manager, Sales) :-
    area_manager(Manager, Country),
    based(Customer, Country),
    sales_to(Customer, Sales).
```

For instance, we might ask for a breakdown of all sales in Scotland by writing the following query:

```
?- breakdown_country(scotland, Sales).
```

The PROLOG interpreter would then reply with the following information:

```
Sales = 10000
```

and then:

```
Sales = 7000.
```

Similarly, if we wanted a breakdown by manager, the following query would be issued:

```
?- breakdown_manager(bloggs, Sales).
```

The system would reply:

```
Sales = 15000
```

and then:

```
Sales = 5000
```

Views

In effect, then, what we are doing in terms of writing the rules above is creating a mechanism for running common queries on our database. These rules are what are known as 'views' in relational database terms. In other words, they express how to form virtual tables from the base information in the database. The first view produces information on sales by country. The second view produces information on sales by manager.

Rules such as these turn a conventional database into a deductive database. A conventional relational database consists of a collection of facts. A deductive database contains not only facts but also rules. This enables it to make deductions, i.e. generate new facts from facts already existing in the database.

PROLOG and the Relational Algebra

Such queries are really a combination of the select, project and join operations of relational algebra discussed in Chapter 2, except that we are not actually creating a new relation to store the result of the query. These operators can however be simulated in PROLOG.

The 'select' operator constructs a horizontal subset of a relation. For example, we might want to select customers where country = 'scotland'.

To incorporate such a facility into our database we would need to write the following rule:

```
select_country(Country) :-
    based(Name, Country),
    assertz(new(Name, Country)).
```

Similarly, a 'project' operator constructs a vertical subset of a relation. For example, project area—manager over manager. This can be done with the following rule:

```
project_manager(Manager) :-
    area_manager(Manager, Country),
    assertz(new(Manager, Country)).
```

Finally, probably the most useful operation, join, produces a new relation from two relations with an attribute in common. For example, join sales—to with based over name giving temp. The rule below implements this idea in PROLOG:

```
join:-
    sales_to(name, Sales),
    based(Name, Country),
    assertz(temp(Name, Sales, Country)).
```

Queries

One implicit assumption underlying conventional relational databases which has been made explicit through the application of logic is the distinction between a closed and an open query instance, a closed query expressed on the sales database might be:

'Does Bloggs manage England?'

This can be expressed in PROLOG as:

```
?- area_manager(bloggs, england).
```

and would evaluate to yes or true in terms of a match with our database.

An open query requires a set of records as a response. Suppose for instance we wish to express the following query on our database:

'list all sales over 7000'

A conventional SQL version of this would be:

```
SELECT customer, qty
FROM sales
WHERE qty > 7000
```

We express this in logic as:

```
?- sales_to(Customer, Qty), Qty > 7000.
```

Suppose, however, that a variant of this query finds that there are no sales of a given order. What does this mean? The conventional interpretation relies on another implicit assumption made explicit by logic work. This assumption, known variously as the 'closed world assumption' or 'negation as failure', states that, in a nondeductive database, any relationship between objects which is not represented explicitly is assumed not to hold.

Integrity Constraints

Since data often contain errors, integrity constraints are used to describe properties which the data need to satisfy for the data to be correct.

Suppose we want to ensure that sales to Scottish companies are all of a certain order. We can represent this as a rule in our database as follows:

```
scottish_sale(Qty) :-
               breakdown_country(scotland, Qty),
               Qty > 7000.
```

That is, 'if customer is a Scottish customer, then the order of the sale should be above 7000'.

Note the rule above could only be used, however, in the sense of listing valid Scottish sales. What we really want is some mechanism whereby those Scottish sales under 7000 are retracted from the database. Here we get into the area of building an interface to a PROLOG database, which unfortunately is outside the scope of this work.

Conclusion

Note that the integrity constraint above uses a rule which we previously defined as being a view on our database. In a logic database the distinction between different types of rules becomes largely irrelevant. A view can be regarded as an integrity constraint and an integrity constraint can be regarded as a special type of view. This is the primary point of the exercise: that logic acts as a uniform formalism for representing a vast array of database concerns, both in terms of conventional databases and databases with deductive facilities.

Problems

1. Describe the components of the predicate calculus.
2. Encode the following information which we might find in a personnel database into predicate calculus notation:
   'Davies is the director of a small software house called Simplesoft. Jones and Evans are analyst/programmers that work for Davies. Jones also has an additional responsibility as the hardware expert for the firm.'
3. Why is the predicate calculus unsuitable for computerization?
4. Assume we gave the following two files in a banking database:

```
CUSTOMERS(name, max_total_balance)
ACCOUNTS(account_no, balance, customer_name)).
```

Write English translations of the following constraints expressed on this database:

∀ = universal quantifier
∃ = existential quantifier
∈ = member of set
COUNT = returns cardinality of set
SUM = returns summative value from set

(a) ∀ a ∈ ACCOUNTS
     ∃ c ∈ CUSTOMERS WHERE
        a.customer_name = c.name

(b) ∀ c ∈ CUSTOMERS
     ∃ a ∈ ACCOUNTS WHERE
        c.name = a.customer_name

(c) ∀ c ∈ CUSTOMERS
        4 > = COUNT (a ∈ ACCOUNTS WHERE a.customer_name = c.name)

(d) ∀ c ∈ CUSTOMERS
        c.max_tot_balance > = SUM a.balance WHERE
        (a ∈ ACCOUNTS AND a.customer_name = c.name)

5. Given the following insurance database:

```
POLICY (policy_no, premium)
LIFE_POLICY (policy_no, age_of_insured)
VEHICLE_POLICY (policy_no, no_claims_bonus)
```

write logic constraints which express the following statements:
(a) There is a unique policy identified by a policy number for each life policy.
(b) There is a unique policy identified by a policy number for each vehicle policy.
(c) Policies are either for life insurance or for vehicle insurance.
(d) Policy numbers assigned to vehicle and life policies are distinct.

6. Express the relational database below as a logic database.

```
CUSTOMERS

Name        Max_total_balance

Bloggs      200
Bilbo       150
Baggins     250

ACCOUNTS

Account_no Balance Customer_name

0101          10      Bloggs
0102          20      Bloggs
0201         100      Bilbo
0202          75      Bilbo
0301         200      Baggins
```

7. Is the database in Problem 6 consistent with the integrity rules expressed in Problem 3?

TWELVE

Conceptual Modelling

Introduction

There has been interest in artificial intelligence–database (AI–DB) integration for over 30 years. Turing's test, originally formulated in 1951, postulated a machine that might emulate human intelligence by accessing and inferencing on a large information base. Many early question-answering, learning and other such systems, such as McCarthy's Advice-Taker (McCorduck, 1978) assumed access to large, possibly shared information bases. Such systems implicitly assumed database capabilities. They did not, however, explicitly address any of the emerging issues in the DB field.

AI–DB integration was addressed specifically in early work in natural language interfaces and intelligent information retrieval. This has blossomed into a number of different areas, some of which we have discussed in this work. There is no doubt that there has been an undoubted increase of interest in AI–DB integration over the last 30 years. This is evident in a number of indicators (Brodie, 1989):

1. The number of papers published—under 10 in 1958, around 25 in 1968, over 60 in 1978, just under 350 in 1988
2. The number of AI–DB projects—36 in 1983, over 350 in 1988
3. The number of conferences, workshops and panels held—more than 30 in the years 1978–88
4. The number of commercial products introduced—over 35 between 1987 and 1988.

The Central Premise

The central premise of this work is neatly summed up in a quote from an article by Michael Brodie, one of the key figures in Expert Database research (Brodie, 1989):

The effective application of Artificial Intelligence (AI) technology and the development of future computing systems require the integration of AI and database (DB) technologies. The integration will benefit both technologies and will substantially advance the state of computing.

He goes on to predict that:

Future computing systems will require AI and DB technology to work together with other technologies. These systems will consist of large numbers of heterogeneous, distributed agents that have varying abilities to work cooperatively. Each will have its own knowledge and reasoning schemes, languages and capabilities. Data, procedures, knowledge and objects in these systems may be shared, incomplete, and inconsistent with other agents, but they will certainly persist and will together form a massive distributed information base. The current trend towards inter-connectivity and inter-operability—one system accessing another via standard interfaces—will evolve into intelligent inter-operability—intelligent cooperation among systems to optimally achieve specified goals.

This is clearly a grandiose scheme for expert database research. It is a scheme, however, which will have to wait some time to achieve fruition, and is hampered by the fact that:

Effective AI–DB integration requires a deep understanding by AI people of what DB technology could offer and by DB people of the requirements of AI systems. This understanding has yet to happen. Unfortunately, there has been little effective communication between AI scientists and their DB colleagues.

The overall aim of this work has been to demonstrate how an effective understanding of both expert systems and database technology is essential for the application developers of the future. In this conclusive chapter we change the emphasis a little from applications to system builders. We consider two ways in which expert database systems have an important role to play in the computer-aided software engineering arena. We begin with a summary description of the place of expert systems as a tool for database design. We then re-examine the data dictionary concept in the light of an ANSI standard information resource dictionary system (IRDS) and discuss an expert database architecture for the IRDS. Finally, we consider some of the problems of distributed database systems and how an object-oriented data model will help in this area.

Expert Systems for Database Design

Logical database design is concerned with determining the contents of a database independently of implementation considerations. Most existing database design techniques have been created for, or adapted to, the relational data model. The two most prominent of such techniques are normalization and entity–relationship diagramming. Both such techniques have acquired a degree of formalization over the last two decades. In spite of this, however, database design is still a complex and lengthy process involving a considerable amount of design expertise. It is for this reason that a number of researchers have begun to investigate the role of expert systems for database design (Bouzeghoub and Gardarin, 1984) (Storey and Goldstein, 1988). The aim is to rebuild one instance of an 'intelligent' CASE tool.

This section considers briefly how such a tool might be built. It does so by considering the technique of entity–relationship diagramming, an offshoot of the entity–relationship model as discussed in Chapter 9. It demonstrates how an initial knowledge base might be built for this activity and then examines the extent to which this expert system might be extended to produce a more practicable CASE tool.

Entity–Relationship Diagramming

An entity–relationship diagram (E–R diagram) is what it says. It is a model of an information system in terms of entities, and the relationships between such entities. The assumption underlying the technique is that there is a 'real world' which can be modelled in terms of entities and relationships. We might refer to this as an entity model. An E–R diagram is a method for representing an entity model in pictorial form (Beynon-Davies, 1989).

Entities and Relationships

An entity may be defined as anything which an enterprise recognizes as being capable of an independent existence and which can be uniquely identified (Howe, 1983). An entity may be an object such as a house or a car or an event such as a house sale or a car service.

A relationship can be defined as an association between two or more entities (Howe, 1983). Hence we might say that a company department is related to company employees in the sense that a department is made up of employees.

We indicate an entity on an entity model by a rectangular box in which is written a meaningful name for the entity. For example,

$$\boxed{\text{EMPLOYEE}}$$

We indicate a relationship between two entities by drawing a labelled line between the relevant boxes on our diagram. For example,

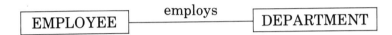

Properties of a Relationship

There are a number of properties of the concept of a relationship which are usually considered important. The most important of these is the degree of a relationship. A relationship can be said to be either a 1:1 (one-to-one) relationship, a $1:M$ (one-to-many) relationship, or an $M:N$ (many-to-many) relationship.

For instance, the relationship between salesmen and customers can be said to be 1:1 if it can be defined in the following way:

A salesman services at most one customer.
A customer may be serviced by at most one salesman.

In contrast, the relationship between salesman and customers is $1:M$ if it is defined as:

A salesman services many customers.
A customer may be serviced by at most one salesman.

Finally, we are approaching a realistic representation of the relationship when we describe it as being $M:N$. That is:

A salesman services many customers.
A customer may be serviced by many salesmen.

We represent the degree of a relationship by drawing a crow's foot on the many end of a relationship.

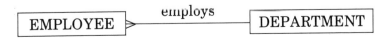

Another important property of a relationship concerns the participation of each entity in the relationship. For some entity we might say that every occurrence of that entity participates in the relationship. For other entities it may be true to say that occurrences of the entity can exist independently of the relationship.

For example, suppose that the employs relationship between an employee and a department can be detailed as follows:

Every employee must be employed by a department.
A department may exist without any employees.

For this relationship we say that membership of employee in the employs relationship is mandatory. In other words, an employee occurrence must participate in the employs relationship. In contrast, the membership of department in the employs relationship is optional. In other words, a department occurrence can exist without participating in the employs relationship.

When an entity's participation is mandatory we draw a dot inside the entity symbol. When it is optional we draw a dot on the relationship line, prior to any crow's foot.

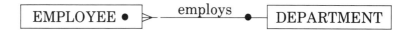

The Knowledge Base

Given that we can draw a diagram in which the degree of the relationship between entities and the participation of each of the entities in the relationship is represented, the knowledge base shown in Fig. 12.1 may be applied to determine the appropriate relational database design.

The knowledge base should be relatively self-explanatory. Rule 6 for instance states that if the relationship between two entities (say WARD and PATIENT) is one-to-many and the many entity is optionally involved in the relationship (i.e. there is at least one empty ward in our hospital) then we should create three tables, one for each entity, and one to cross-reference wards with patients. We should also build the relationship table as a compound identifier of the ward identifier and the patients identifier. Such as, for instance,

```
WARDS(ward_no, ...)
PATIENTS(patient_no,...)
STAYS(ward_no, patient_no, ...)
```

```
1: IF     degree1          IS one
   AND degree2             IS one
   AND participation1      IS mandatory
   AND participation2      IS mandatory
   THEN   structure is one_table

2: IF     degree1          IS one
   AND degree2             IS one
   AND participation1      IS optional
   AND participation2      IS mandatory
   THEN   structure        IS two_tables
   AND posting             IS mandatory_to_optional

3: IF     degree1          IS one
   AND degree2             IS one
   AND participation1      IS mandatory
   AND participation2      IS optional
   THEN   structure        IS two_tables
   AND posting             IS mandatory_to_optional

4: IF     degree1          IS one
   AND degree2             IS one
   AND participation1      IS optional
   AND participation2      IS optional
   THEN   structure        IS three_tables
   AND posting             IS entities_to_relationship

5: IF     degree1          IS one
   AND degree2             IS many
   AND participation1      IS optional
   OR  participation1      IS mandatory
   AND participation2      IS mandatory
   THEN   structure        IS two_tables
   AND posting             IS one_to_many

6: IF     degree1          IS one
   AND degree2             IS many
   AND participation1      IS optional
   OR  participation1      IS mandatory
   AND participation2      IS optional
   THEN   structure        IS three_tables
   AND posting             IS entities_to_relationship

7: IF     degree1          IS many
   AND degree2             IS many
   THEN   structure        IS three_tables
   AND posting             IS entities_to_relationship
```

Figure 12.1.   A knowledge base

Extensions

The knowledge base above, although useful as an illustration, is clearly an over-simplification of the problem of database design. It is amenable, however, to improvement in a number of directions.

For instance, E–R diagramming is a technique in itself which requires practice. A more productive CASE tool of this nature would probably have a natural-language-like front end which would handle all interactions with database designers, whether they were computing professionals or even end-users (see Fig. 12.2). Users, for example, might enter phrases such as 'salesmen and technicians are employees', 'a salesman has a name and address', or 'a salesman services a customer' and the expert system would parse these phrases into entities, relationships and attributes. The expert system would then prompt the user for information about the degree and participation of each of the entities in the relationships of the ongoing entity model. As it goes along, the expert system would check the internal consistency of this model and users would be able to continually ask questions as to the rationale for the decisions made by the expert system. There might even be the possibility of allowing the user to choose between a number of alternative design decisions at various points in the development process.

A Standard Information Resource Dictionary System

Historically, data management has concentrated on developing effective database systems through the application of database management systems (DBMSs). An integral part of any DBMS is a repository of information known as the data dictionary. The data dictionary contains descriptions of operational databases. It stores meta-data which describe the operational structure of files in subject databases.

In recent years, the scope of the data dictionary concept has been continually expanded. Data dictionary systems (DDSs) now include information about programs, users, hardware and corporate information strategy (Navathe and Kerschberg, 1986). This enhanced notion of a DDS is commonly referred to as an information resource dictionary system (IRDS). An IRDS is a centralized repository of data about all relevant information resources used within an organization.

In 1984 ANSI accepted a draft standard for the IRDS concept (Goldfine, 1985). The standard IRDS was designed to satisfy a number of objectives:

1. It should contain the major capabilities to be found in contemporary DDS.
2. It should be possible to tailor the IRDS to the demands of particular products and sites.

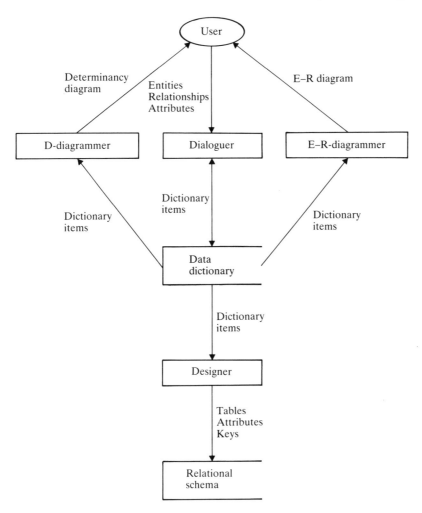

Figure 12.2.   A database design tool

3. It should be portable across a wide range of different hardware and
    software environments.

   The section describes the architecture of the IRDS standard and
discusses the role of expert database systems in this area.

The Architecture

The IRDS standard specifies a core system containing the basic dictionary facilities found in most DDSs. Around this core it further specifies a

collection of independent, optional modules which extend the functionality of the core. These modules are:

1. A module to provide an increased level of security
2. An application program interface
3. Documentation support for standard DBMS.

The IRDS architecture is based on a semantic data model known as the entity–relationship model. In this model, the user perceives the dictionary as being made up of entities, relationships and attributes. All relationships in the IRDS are binary. Entities may be related to themselves. Attributes may be associated either with entities or with relationships.

The Core

The IRDS core is made up of two parts: the information resource dictionary (IRD) and the IRD schema. The structure of both the IRD and the IRD schema is defined in terms of the entity–relationship model. The IRD is made up of entities, attributes and relationships that are instances of the corresponding IRD schema entity-types, relationship-types and attribute-types. Thus, the IRD may contain the data PERSONNEL-RECORD which is an instance of the entity-type RECORD, which in turn is an instance of the meta-entity-type ENTITY-TYPE.

Entity-types

The IRD schema contains 12 entity-types categorized as either data, process or external.
DATA
   FILE, RECORD, ELEMENT, DOCUMENT, BIT-STRING,
   CHARACTER-STRING, FIXED-POINT, FLOAT

EXTERNAL
   USER

PROCESS
   SYSTEM, PROGRAM, MODULE

Relationship-types

All relationship-types in the core system are binary and are named according to the entity-types that participate in the relationship. For example, SYSTEM-CONTAINS-PROGRAM is a valid relationship-type. Integrity constraints in the IRDS are defined in terms of which entity-types can participate in which relationships. Some valid relationship-types are given below:

CONTAINS, PROCESSES, RESPONSIBLE-FOR, RUNS,
GOES-TO, CALLS, DERIVED-FROM, REPRESENTED-AS

Attribute-types

Attribute-types are divided into two major classes: those that are entity-related and those that are relationship-related. Some attributes are common to all entity-types. For instance, DATE-CREATED, DESCRIPTION and COMMENTS. Other attribute-types are associated with just one or a few entity-types. For example, NUMBER-OF-RECORDS is unique to the FILE entity-type. ACCESS-METHOD is an attribute of relevance to relationship-types such as SYSTEM-PROCESSES-FILE, PROGRAM-PROCESSES-FILE, and MODULE-PROCESSES-FILE.

Usage

The IRDS can be used in a number of different ways to control and monitor the data needed to support organizational behaviour. An important output from the IRDS, for instance, is the impact-of-change report. This report will list all entities affected by a change to one or more other entities in the system. Other control facilities include:

1. Versioning. Allowing descriptions of multiple versions of the same entity such as a PROGRAM.
2. Life-cycle phasing. Allowing each entity to be assigned to a phase in the life-cycle. The IRDS provides integrity rules governing the movement of entities from one phase to another.
3. Quality control. A number of quality indicators can be assigned to entities.
4. Views. Different users can be given different perspectives on the data dictionary.

Expansion of the Data Dictionary Role

The IRDS standard is important for the future of commercial computing for a number of reasons, all of which centre around the expansion of the

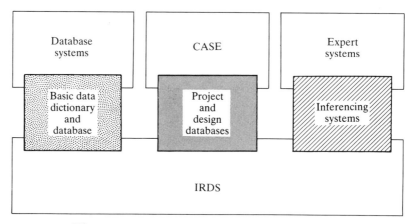

Figure 12.3. Role of the standard IRDS

data dictionary concept. Data dictionaries, for instance, look like being the major mechanism by which third-party software will be connected to DBMS. Data dictionaries will also offer the means to connect various different databases running under different DBMSs, perhaps even on different hardware. Data dictionaries of the future may even act in the capacity of a store for application-specific logic (see Fig. 12.3). Any standard in this area, albeit of a small common core, is therefore destined to enhance the possibilities in all these areas and many more.

The IRDS as an Expert Database System

A proposal has been made for a relational implementation of the IRDS (Dolk and Kirsch, 1987). As we discussed in Chapter 9, however, implementing the IRDS as a relational database would involve a substantial loss of knowledge. Far better to implement the IRDS as an expert database system using an underlying semantic data model such as the entity–relationship model.

For example, the IRDS standard has a life-cycle phase facility. This facility allows an organization to define life-cycle phases corresponding to the methodology used by the organization. Each life-cycle phase so defined is represented as a meta-entity in the IRD schema. Every life-cycle phase belongs to one of three phase classes:

1. Uncontrolled—these represent non-operational phases of a system life cycle such as analysis and design.
2. Controlled—designed to be used for defining entities in the IRD schema that are operational.

3. Archived—used to document entities no longer in use.

The IRDS standard enforces a set of integrity rule for entities in the controlled or archived phases. These rules are defined on a specified hierarchy of entity-types and relationship-types. The following list represents the hierarchy of entity-types:

> SYSTEM
> PROGRAM
> MODULE
> FILE
> DOCUMENT
> RECORD
> ELEMENT

The highest in the hierarchy is the first entity-type in the list, and the lowest is the last. CONTAINS and PROCESSES represent the two relationships available to be defined on this hierarchy. FILE-CONTAINS-RECORD and PROGRAM-PROCESSES-FILE are thus valid relationships for phase control.

The general integrity rule for entities in a controlled life-cycle phase is:

> An entity can be in the controlled life-cycle phase only if all entities whose types are below its type in the hierarchy and that are connected to it with the available relationships are also in the controlled life-cycle phase.

In other words, if an entity such as a program is to be moved to the controlled phase, and this entity is associated with other entities whose types are lower in the hierarchy, such as a file, then either:

1. All the related entities must be in the controlled phase, or
2. All related entities not in the controlled phase must be moved to the controlled phase before the program entity can be moved there.

Here we have an effective mechanism which demonstrates the possibilities for controlling the software development process by the application of a semantic data model.

Distributed Database Systems

A distributed database system (DDB) is a database system which involves a number of sites connected together by some form of communication network. Each site in the network can be considered as a database system in its own right. The fundamental aim of a DDB is to allow a user located at any site to access data stored anywhere on the network.

This section reviews some of the overall objectives of DDBs and discusses some of the advantages and disadvantages of such systems. It then discusses a novel architecture for a distributed database management system.

Objectives of a DDB

There are a number of objectives which the ideal DDB should fulfil:

- Location transparency. This means that details of the actual location of data should be hidden from the user of the DDB. In other words, the user of the DDB should be able to act in all respects as if the data he requires is stored at his own local site.
- Data fragmentation. This means that any given file in the system can be divided up into fragments and such fragments located at various different points in the network. For example, a multinational might wish to maintain a global personnel file but for reasons of performance decides to locate national subsets of this file at its local offices around the world.
- Fragmentation transparency. This becomes an associated objective to location transparency. Users in our multinational company which employs a fragmented database should be able to express queries on the global personnel file in exactly the same way as they would for, say, British employees. Data fragmentation and fragmentation transparency are two of the most important reasons why DDBs are almost invariably relational. This is because, unlike the data structures of a hierarchical or network database, relations are relatively easy to fragment and recombine.
- Data replication. Another objective for a DDB is to be able to support data replication, i.e. the siting of various copies of data around the network. At first sight, this would seem in many ways to be a direct infringement of the original rationale behind the database concept—to avoid data redundancy. The main advantage of such replication is that queries on a replicated database can be directed to the nearest copy in the network. This improves retrieval performance. The disadvantage is that to support replication transparency updates to the DDB must be directed to all appropriate copies.

Advantages of a DDB

Building and maintaining a distributed database system is no easy task. What therefore prompts organizations to go distributed? Some of the advantages listed below explain this in part:

- Reflecting organizational structure. Most large enterprises are usually logically and physically distributed: logically into departments and divisions, physically into offices and factories. Distributing a system can more clearly reflect the way in which a company is organized. Data can be sited where it is needed and where local control can be exercised over it.
- Incremental growth. A major reason for distributing a system is that it allows an easy upgrade path. A distributed system can grow more gracefully than a nondistributed one. Rather than purchasing a larger replacement machine to handle growing company information requirements, machines can be added to the company information network when and as needed.
- Reliability. A distributed system frequently offers greater reliability than a centralized system. This is because it can frequently continue to function even if one or a number of sites go down on the network.

Disadvantages of a DDB

Most of the problems of DDBs arise from the fact that long-haul networks are very slow. Thus an overall objective of any DDB must be to reduce the amount of data transmission to a minimum. As a consequence, the software which manages a DDB must be of an order more complex than a local database manager. For instance, the query optimizer in a DDB must be a lot more sophisticated than a conventional optimizer. It must know how to handle and exploit the fragmentation and replication implemented in any particular DDB.

Types of DDB

The term 'distributed database system' can be applied to a number of systems differing in various respects. One classic distinction revolves around the degree of homogeneity of the DDBMS software. At one extreme we can describe a DDB as homogeneous if the same DBMS is running on various machines in the network. At the other extreme we can describe a DDB as being heterogeneous if a number of different DBMSs are running at various points in the network. Clearly, a DDBMS for a homogeneous environment is easier to implement than one for a heterogeneous environment.

Another dimension along which we might compare distributed database systems is on the degree of local autonomy. At one extreme we may have a DDB in which none of the nodes have any autonomy. They all act as servers to a global database schema. At the other extreme we have the concept of a federated database system (sometimes referred to as a multidatabase system). Here, each node in the network is an independent, and autonomous database system. Each node, however, can cooperate with other nodes to build a distributed database schema.

The Growth of Distributed Systems

A recent report by OVUM on the future of databases predicts that the growth of distributed database systems will climb steadily into the early 1990s (OVUM Report, 1988). Work on DBMSs for handling DDBs is progressing apace. Companies like Oracle and RTI (Ingres) already have a capacity for homogeneous distributed databases. Ingres has a limited capacity for heterogeneous environments. Much more research and development work needs to take place, however, particularly into federated structures, before we can feel confident of achieving some of the objectives discussed in this section.

An Object-oriented DDBMS

Because of some of the fundamental features of the approach, the object-oriented data model seems ideally suited for managing distributed applications. It is possible to imagine, for instance, a distributed database manager built using the object-oriented approach. Each node in a distributed system would be built as an object in the DBMS, that is as a package of data structures and rules. Such a package would describe not only the data held at each site but also information about communication protocols, characteristics of the native DBMS, and so on.

This would mean that any query coming from the user would be translated by a manager object into a set of messages to be directed at appropriate node objects. The node objects would trigger in-built procedures, methods or sets of rules, and transmit the results back to the manager object as messages. The manager object would resolve the incoming messages to transmit a transparent response for the user.

Conclusion

To conclude let us review some of the fundamental themes underlying the expert database endeavour:

- Database systems were originally developed to handle the problems of manipulating large fact bases.
- Knowledge base systems were originally developed as a reaction against the ideas underlying the notion of a general theorem prover.
- Because of an increasing demand for functionality, database systems are incorporating ideas originally developed in artificial intelligence.
- The first expert systems were developed in the technical and scientific arena. Such systems needed large rule bases, but relatively small fact bases.
- Expert systems have migrated into the business arena. Business expert systems are increasingly seeing a need for data management facilities.
- The integration of AI and DB technology is taking place on two levels: integrating existing tools and developing new, revolutionary architectures.
- The integration of AI and DB will enhance both base applications and system builders.
- The integration of AI and DB will undoubtedly enhance future computing.

Problems

1. Draw an E–R diagram of the database in Fig. 2.7.
2. How does the E–R diagram differ from a semantic net drawn for this database?
3. What do you think are the degrees of the following relationships taken from the IRDS schema:
   (a) SYSTEM-CONTAINS-PROGRAM
   (b) PROGRAM-PROCESSES-FILE
   (c) PROGRAM-CALLS-MODULE
4. Why do you think the IRDS was expressed in terms of the entity–relationship data model rather than the relational model?

5. How might the database design rule base be enhanced with some of the developments discussed for POSTQUEL in Chapter 6?
6. What are the objectives of a distributed database system?
7. Explain the difference between a homogeneous, a heterogeneous and a federated database system.

Glossary

Abstract data type A programming abstraction. A package of data structures and procedures.

Abstraction The process of modelling 'real-world' concepts in a computational medium.

Aggregation The process by which a higher-level object is used to group together a number of lower-level objects.

Alerter A rule mechanism embedded in a database designed to notify a user of a change in the state of the database.

Artificial intelligence The discipline devoted to producing computing systems that perform tasks which would require intelligence if done by a human being.

Assertion A rule expressed on a database to maintain validity. Otherwise known as a fact. A proposition whose validity is accepted.

Association A form of abstraction in which a relationship between objects is considered a higher-level set object.

Attribute The property of an object. A column in a relation.

Backtracking The process of backing up through a series of inferences in the face of unacceptable results.

Backward chaining An inference mechanism which works from a goal and attempts to satisfy a set of initial conditions. Also referred to as goal-directed or data-directed chaining/reasoning.

CASE Computer-aided/assisted software engineering.

Classification A form of abstraction in which a number of objects are considered instances of a higher-level object.

Conflict resolution The process by which a rule interpreter decides which of a range of possible rules to fire.

Data model An architecture for data, made up of three components: a set of data structures; a set of data operators; a set of inherent integrity rules.

Database A structured pool of organizational data.

DBMS Database management system. A system which manages all interactions with a database.

Declarative knowledge Also known as factual knowledge. A form of knowledge which makes assertions about the meaning of objects and the relationships between objects.

Deduction Reasoning from theories to facts.

Deductive database system   A term normally used to describe a logic database with the ability to perform inference.

Domain   A bounded area of knowledge. The pool of values which may be assigned to an attribute.

Enhanced database system   A database system enhanced with a deductive component.

Enhanced expert system   An expert system enhanced with data management facilities.

Entity   Some aspects of the real world which have an independent existence and can be uniquely identified.

Entity integrity   An inherent integrity rule of the relational model which states that there must always be a primary key of a table.

Entity–relationship model   A data model due to Chen which models the world in terms of entities and relationships between entities.

Expert database system   An ambiguous term used in a number of different senses:

1.   A system formed from the combination of an expert system with a database system.
2.   An expert system enhanced with data management facilities or a database system enhanced with a deductive component.
3.   An advanced database system employing new architectures for knowledge representation.
4.   Any system lying at the intersection of AI and database work.

Expert system   A computer system that achieves high levels of performance in areas that for human beings require large amounts of expertise.

Expert system shell   An expert system stripped of its domain-specific knowledge.

Explanation facility   The mechanisms for justifying or rationalizing the actions of a knowledge base system.

Foreign key   Attributes in a relation which reference other keys in a database.

Forward chaining   An inference mechanism which works from a set of initial conditions to a goal. Also referred to as data-directed chaining.

Frame   A knowledge representation scheme that describes objects in terms of slots and fillers.

Generalization   A form of abstraction in which a higher-level object is formed by emphasizing the similarities between a number of lower-level objects.

Induction   Reasoning from facts to theories.

Inference The process of generating conclusions from conditions or new facts from known facts.

Inference engine That part of an expert system which makes inferences from the knowledge base.

Inheritance The transference of properties from ancestor objects to descendant objects.

Instantiation The process of binding values to variables.

Integrity Maintaining the validity or logical consistency of a database.

Integrity constraint A rule for maintaining integrity.

Interdependent ES/DB Independent expert system and database system connected together by a common data channel.

Join An operator of the relational algebra.

Knowledge base A collection of facts and rules which represent the knowledge in a particular domain.

Knowledge base management system A system for handling knowledge modelled on the lines of a database management system.

Knowledge base system (KBS) A system containing knowledge which can perform tasks which require intelligence if done by human beings.

Knowledge engineer A person, analogous to the systems analyst in traditional computing, who builds a KBS.

Knowledge representation The process of mapping the knowledge of some domain into a computational medium.

LISP A functional language developed for list processing. The favoured language of the US AI community.

Logic programming Using symbolic logic as a programming language. A branch of AI devoted to the use of PROLOG.

Natural language interface An English-like interface to a database.

Object Some aspect of the real world. A software construct encapsulating data and procedures.

Object–attribute–value triplet The major component of a production rule.

Object-oriented database A database system founded in an object-oriented data model.

Object-oriented programming A branch of AI devoted to the idea of building systems out of frame-like objects.

Predicate calculus A form of logic mechanized as PROLOG.

Primary key The identifier for each tuple in a relation.

Production rule An if–then rule having a set of conditions and a set of consequent conclusions.

Program-data independence   The immunity of applications to changes in the structure of a database.

Projection   An operator of the relational algebra.

PROLOG   A logic programming language. The favoured language of much of the European AI community and the Japanese fifth-generation project.

Referential integrity   An inherent integrity constraint of the relational model. A foreign key must either be null, or the primary key of a related table.

Relation   A disciplined table. The fundamental data structure of the relational data model.

Relational algebra   The manipulative part of the relational data model.

Relational calculus   An alternative to the relational algebra. Based on the predicate calculus.

Relational model   A data model originally invented by E. F. Codd.

Relationship   An association between two or more entities.

Selection   An operator of the relational algebra. Produces a subset of rows from a table.

Semantic data model   A data model which has a range of richer constructs for modelling the real world.

Semantic nets   A network which incorporates meaning. Taken originally from work undertaken in cognitive psychology.

Semantic query optimization   Query optimization strategies that employ heuristics.

Shell   See expert system shell.

Slot   The major component of a frame.

SQL   Structured query language. A query language based on the relational calculus.

Table   See relation.

Trigger   A rule mechanism embedded in a database designed to effect transitional changes to a database.

Tuple   A row in a relation.

Working memory   That part of an expert system designed to store temporary results of inferencing.

References and Further Reading

Abarbanel, M. and M. D. Williams, 'A relational representation for knowledge bases'. In Kerschberg, 1986.

Addis, T. R. (1987) *Designing Knowledge Base Systems*, Kogan Page, London.

Alty, J. L. and M. J. Coombs (1984) *Expert Systems: Concepts and Examples*, NCC Publications, Manchester.

Al-Zobaidie, A. and J. B. Grimson (1987) 'Expert systems and database systems: how can they serve each other?', *Expert Systems*, **4**(1), 30–7.

Appleton, D. S. (1986) 'Rule-based data resource management', *Datamation*, **32**(9), 86–9.

Bachmann, C. W. (1973) 'The programmer as navigator', *Communications of ACM*, **16**, 47–50.

Barr, A. and E. A. Feigenbaum (1982) *The Handbook of Artificial Intelligence* (3 vols), MIT Press, Cambridge, Mass.

Beech, D. (1989) 'New life for SQL', *Datamation*, **34**(26), 29–36.

Beynon-Davies, P. (1987) 'Software engineering and knowledge engineering: unhappy bedfellows?', *Computer Bulletin*, **3**(4), 9–11.

Beynon-Davies, P. (1989) *Information Systems Development*, Macmillan, London.

Bharath, R. (1986) *An Introduction to PROLOG*, TAB Books, New York.

Bing Yao, S. (ed.) (1985) *Principles of Database Design, Vol. 1: Logical Organizations*, Prentice-Hall, Englewood Cliffs, N.J.

Bond, A. (ed.) (1982) *Machine Intelligence, Infotech State of the Art Report 9*, MIT Press, Cambridge, Mass.

Bonnet, A., J. P. Haton and J. M. Truong-Ngoc (1988) *Expert Systems: Principles and Practice*, Prentice-Hall, Englewood Cliffs, N.J.

Bouzeghoub, M. and G. Gardarin (1984) 'The design of an expert system for database design'. In Gardarin and Gellenbe, 1984.

Bowers, D. S. (1989) 'From database to information base: some questions of semantics and constraints', *Information and Software Technology*, Summer.

Brachman, R. J. (1983) 'What IS-A is and isn't: an analysis of the taxonomic links in semantic networks', *Computer*, October, 30–6.

Brachman, R. J. and H. J. Levesque (1986) 'What makes a knowledge base knowledgeable?: a view of databases from the knowledge level'. In Kerschberg, 1986.

Brachman, R. J. and H. J. Levesque (1986) 'Tales from the far side of KRYPTON: lessons for expert database systems from knowledge representation'. In Kerschberg, 1986.

Brereton, O. P. and P. Singleton (1985) 'A facts and rules based approach to generalised attribute management'. In McDermid, 1985.

Brodie, M. L. (1984) 'On the development of data models'. In Brodie, 1984.

Brodie, M. L. (1989) 'Future intelligent information systems: AI and database technologies working together'. In Mylopoulos and Brodie, 1989.

Brodie, M. L., J. Mylopoulos, T. W. Schmidt (eds) (1984) *On Conceptual Modelling: Perspectives from Artificial Intelligence, Databases and Programming Languages*, Springer-Verlag, Berlin.

Buchanan, B. G. and E. A. Feigenbaum (1978) 'Dendral and meta-dendral: their applications dimension', *Artificial Intelligence*, **11**(1), 5–24.

Chen, P. P. S. (1976) 'The entity–relationship model—towards a unified view of data', *ACM Transactions on Database Systems*, **1**, 9–36.

Chen, P. P. S. (1980) *The Entity–Relationship Approach to Systems Analysis and Design*, North-Holland, Amsterdam.

Clocksin, W. F. (1987) 'A Prolog primer', *Byte*, **12**(9), 147–58.

Clocksin, W. F. and C. S. Mellish (1981) *Programming in Prolog*, Springer-Verlag, Berlin.

Codd, E. F. (1970) 'A relational model for large shared data banks', *Communications of ACM*, **13**(6), 377–87.

Codd, E. F. (1979) 'Extending the database relational model to capture more meaning', *ACM Transactions on Database Systems*, **4**(4), 397–434.

Codd, E. F. (1985) 'Is your relational database management system really relational? An evaluation scheme', *ORACLE Users Conference*, San Jose, Calif.

Codd, E. F. (1988a) 'Fatal flaws in SQL', *Datamation*, **34**(16), 45–8.

Codd, E. F. (1988b) 'Fatal flaws in SQL, Part 2', *Datamation*, **34**(17), 71–4.

Date, C. J. (1986) *An Introduction to Database Systems* (Vol. 1, 4th edn), Addison-Wesley, Reading, Mass.

Date, C. J. (1987) 'Where SQL falls short', *Datamation*, **33**(9), 83–6.

Debenham, J. K. (1985) 'Knowledge base design', *Australian Computer Journal*, **17**(1), 42–8.

Debenham, J. K. (1988) 'Expert systems: an information processing perspective'. In Quinlan, 1988.

Delcambre, L. M. and J. N. Etheredge (1989) 'The relational production language: a production language for relational databases'. In Kerschberg, 1989.

De Salvo, D. A., A. E. Glamm and J. Liebowitz (1987) 'Structured design of an expert system prototype at the National Archives'. In Silverman, 1987.

Dolk, D. R. and R. A. Kirsch (1987) 'A relational information resource dictionary system', *Communications of ACM*, **30**(1), 48–61.

Duda, R. O. and J. G. Gaschnig (1981) 'Knowledge-based expert systems come of age', *Byte*, **6**(9), 238–81.

Durham, T. (1988) 'Putting some muscle behind a glossy front', *Computing*, 28 January.

Eisenberg, J. and J. Hill (1984) 'Using natural language systems on personal computers', *Byte*, **9**(1), 226–38.

Elmasri, R. and S. B. Navathe (1989) *Fundamentals of Database Systems*, Benjamin Cummings, Redwood City, Calif.

Erman, L. D., F. Hayes-Roth, V. Lesser and D. Reddy (1980) 'The HEARSAY-II Speech Understanding System. Integrating Knowledge to Resolve Uncertainty', *Computing Surveys*, **12**(2).

Feigenbaum, E. A. (1977) 'The art of artificial intelligence: themes and case studies of knowledge engineering', *IJCAI*, **5**, 1014–29.

Feigenbaum, E. A. and P. McCorduck (1984) *The 5th Generation: Artificial Intelligence and Japan's Computer Challenge to the World*, Michael Joseph, London.

Florentin, J. J. (1987) 'KEE', *Expert Systems*, **4**(2), 118–247.

Forsyth, R. (ed.) *Expert Systems: Principles and Case Studies*, Chapman and Hall, London.

Fox, M. S. 'Beyond the knowledge level'. In Kerschberg, 1986.

Frost, R. A. (1982) 'Binary-relational storage structures', *The Computer Journal*, **25**(3), 358–67.

Frost, R. A. (1983) 'SCHEMAL: yet another conceptual schema definition language', *The Computer Journal*, **26**(3), 228–34.

Frost, R. A. (1986) *Introduction to Knowledge-base Systems*, Collins, London.

Furtado, A. L. and C. M. O. Moura (1986) 'Expert helpers to data-based information systems'. In Kerschberg, 1986.

Furtado, A. L. and E. J. Neuhold (1986) *Formal Techniques for Database Design*, Springer-Verlag, Berlin.

Gallaire, H. and J. Minker (eds) (1978) *Logic and Databases*, Plenum Press, New York.

Gardarin, G. (1984) 'Towards the fifth generation of data management systems'. In Gardarin and Gellenbe, 1984.

Gardarin, G. and E. Gellenbe (1984) *New Applications of Database Systems*, Academic Press, London.

Gaschnig, J. (1982) 'Prospector: an expert system for mineral exploitation'. In Bond, 1982.

Goldfine, A. (1985) 'The information resource dictionary system', *Proc. 4th Entity–Relationship Conf.*, IEEE Press, 114–22.

Goodall, A. (1983) *The Guide to Expert Systems*, Learned Information, Cambridge.

Gray, P. (1985) *Logic, Algebra, and Databases*, Ellis Horwood, Chichester.

Hammer, M. and S. B. Zdonik (1980) 'Knowledge-based query processing', *Proc. 6th VLDB Conf.*, Montreal, Canada, 137–47.

Harris, L. R. (1984) 'Experience with INTELLECT: artificial intelligence technology transfer', *AI Magazine*, **5**(1), 43–50.

Hayes-Roth, F., D. Waterman and D. B. Lenat (eds) (1983) *Building Expert Systems*, Addison-Wesley, Reading, Mass.

Hofstadter, D. R. (1979) *Gödel, Escher and Bach: an eternal golden braid*, Penguin, London.

Howe, D. R. (1983) *Data Analysis for Data Base Design*, Edward Arnold, London.

Israel, D. (1986) 'Knowledge bases and databases'. In Brodie *et al.*, 1984.

Jackson, P. (1986) *Introduction to Expert Systems*, Addison-Wesley, Wokingham.

Jarke, M. and J. Koch (1984) 'Query optimisation in database systems', *Computer Surveys*, **16**(2), 112–52.

Jarke, M. and Y. Vassiliou (1984a) 'Coupling expert systems with database management systems'. In Reitman, 1984.

Jarke, M. and Y. Vassiliou (1984b) 'Databases and expert systems: opportunities and architectures for integration'. In Gardarin and Gellenbe, 1984.

Johnston, R. (1986) 'Early applications get user approval', *Expert Systems User*, **2**(4).

Keller, R. (1987) *Expert System Technology – development and application*, Yourdon Press, New York.

Kerschberg, L. (ed.) (1986) *Expert Database Systems. Proceedings 1st International Conference*, Benjamin Cummings, Redwood City, Calif.

Kerschberg, L. (ed.) (1987) 'Expert database systems', *Computer Bulletin*, **3**(2), 7–16.

Kerschberg, L. (ed.) (1989) *Expert Database Systems. Proceedings 2nd International Conference*, Benjamin Cummings, Redwood City, Calif.

Khan, M. and A. Long (1989) *Bridging the Gap between AI and*

Conventional Computing Systems: Integrating Expert Systems and DBMS, ARIES Club, City of London Polytechnic.

Kim, W. and F. Lochovsky (1988) *Object-Oriented Languages, Applications and Databases*, Addison-Wesley, Reading, Mass.

King, J. J. (1981) 'QUIST: A System for Semantic Query Optimisation in Relational Databases', *IEEE Software*, **2**(1), 510–17.

King, R. (1986) 'A database management system based on an object-oriented model'. In Kerschberg, 1986.

King, R. 'My cat is object-oriented'. In Kim and Lochovsky, 1988.

King, R. and D. McLeod (1985) 'Semantic Data Models'. In Bing Yao, 1985.

Klahr, P. and D. A. Waterman (eds) (1986) *Expert Systems: Techniques, Tools and Applications*, Addison-Wesley, Reading, Mass.

Kowalski, R., (1979a) 'Algorithm = logic + control', *Communications of ACM*, **22**(7), 424–36.

Kowalski, R. (1979b) *Logic for Problem Solving*, North-Holland, Amsterdam.

Kowalski, R. (1984) 'AI and software engineering', *Datamation*, **30**(18), 21–8.

Kowalski, R. (1985) 'Logic programming', *Byte*, **10**(8), 161–76.

Kowalski, R., F. Sadri and P. Soper (1987) 'Integrity checking in deductive databases'. *Proc. 13th VLDB Conference*, Brighton.

Kowalski, R., D. Lenat, E. Soloway, M. Stonebraker and A. Walker (1989) 'Knowledge management'. In Kerschberg, 1989.

Lassez, C. (1987) 'Constraint logic programming', *Byte*, **12**(9), 171–6.

Lehner, P. E. and S. W. Barth (1985) 'Expert systems on microcomputers', *Expert Systems*, **2**(4), 12–16.

LEONARDO manuals. Version 3.18 (1989) Creative Logic, Brunel Science Park.

Levesque, H. V. (1986) 'Making believers out of computers', *Artificial Intelligence*, **30**, 81–108.

Lindsay, R. K., B. G. Buchanan, E. A. Feigenbaum and J. Lederburg (1980) *Applications of Artificial Intelligence for Organic Chemistry: the DENDRAL Project*, McGraw-Hill, New York.

Lloyd, J. W. (1983) 'An introduction to deductive database systems', *The Australian Computer Journal*, **15**(2), 52–7.

McCorduck, D. (1978) *Machines Who Think*, Freeman, New York.

McDermid, J. (ed.) (1985) *Integrated Project Support Environments*, Peter Peregrinus, Cambridge.

McDermott, J. (1980) 'R1: an expert in the computer systems domain', *Proc. American Association for AI Conference*, University of Berkeley, 269–71.

McLeod, D. and R. King (1980) 'Applying a semantic data model'. In Chen, 1980.

Malley, C. V. (1986) 'A knowledge-based approach to query optimisation'. In Kerschberg, 1986.

Maney, T. and I. Reid (1986) *A Management Guide to Artificial Intelligence*, Paradigm, London.

Martin, W. A. and R. J. Fateman (1971) 'The MACSYMA system', *Proc. 2nd Symposium on Symbolic and Algebraic Manipulation*, Los Angeles, 59–75.

Martins, G. R. (1984) 'The overselling of expert systems', *Datamation*, **30**(18), 30–2.

Minsky, M. (1975) 'A framework for representing knowledge'. In P. H. Winston (ed.), *The Psychology of Computer Vision*, McGraw-Hill, New York.

Missikoff, M. and G. Wiederhold (1986) 'Towards a unified approach for expert and database systems'. In Kerschberg, 1986.

Morgenstern, M. (1983) 'Active databases as a paradigm for enhanced computing environments', *Proc. 9th Int. VLDB Conference*, Florence, 34–42.

Morgenstern, M., A. Borgida, C. Lassez, D. Maier and G. Wiederhold (1989) 'Constraint-based systems: knowledge about data'. In Kerschberg, 1989.

Mylopoulos, J. (1989) 'On knowledge base management systems'. In Mylopoulos and Brodie, 1989.

Mylopoulos, J. and M. Brodie (1989) *Readings in Artificial Intelligence and Databases*, Morgan Kaugmann, New York.

Mylopoulos, J., P. A. Bernstein, H. K. T. Wong (1989) 'A language facility for designing database-intensive applications'. In Mylopoulos and Brodie, 1989.

Napheys, B. and Herkimer (1989) 'A look at loosely-coupled Prolog database systems'. In Kerschberg, 1989.

Navathe, S. B. (1989) *Fundamentals of database systems*, Addison-Wesley, Reading, Mass.

Navathe, S. B. and L. Kerschberg (1986) 'The role of data dictionaries in information resource management', *Information and Management*, **10**, 21–46.

Nilsson, N. J. (1980) *Principles of Artificial Intelligence*, Tioga, Palo Alto, Calif.

Osborn, S. L. and T. E. Heaven (1986) 'The design of a relational database system with abstract data types for domains', *ACM Transactions on Database Systems*, **11**(3), 357–73.

OVUM Report (1988) *The Future of Databases*, OVUM Press, London.

Peckham, J. and F. Maryanski (1988) 'Semantic data models', *ACM Computing Surveys*, **20**(3), 153–89.

Quinlan, J. R. (ed.) (1988) *Applications of Expert Systems* (Vol. 1), Addison-Wesley, Sydney.

Reiter, R., H. Gallaire, J. J. King, J. Mylopoulos and B. L. Webber (1983) 'A panel on AI and databases', *Proc. 8th International Conference on AI*, Karlsruhe, W. Germany, 1199–1205.

Reitman, W. (1984) *Artificial Intelligence Applications for Business*, Ablex Publishing, New York.

Rich, E. (1983) *Artificial Intelligence*, McGraw-Hill, Singapore.

Rich, E. (1984), 'Natural language interfaces', *Computer*, September, 39–47.

Roussopoulos, N. and J. Mylopoulos (1989) 'Using semantic networks for database management'. In Mylopoulos and Brodie, 1989.

Sergot, M. J., F. Sadri, A. Kowalski, F. Kriwaczek and H. T. Cory (1986) 'The British Nationality Act as a logic program', *Communications of ACM*, **29**(5), 370–86.

Shepherd, A. and L. Kerschberg (1986) 'Constraint management in expert database systems'. In Kerschberg, 1986.

Shipman, D. W. (1981) 'The functional data model and the data language DAPLEX', *ACM Transactions on Database Systems*, **6**(1), 140–73.

Shortliffe, E. H. (1976) *Computer-based Medical Consultations: MYCIN*, Elsevier, New York.

Silverman, B. G. (ed.) (1987) *Expert Systems for Business*, Addison-Wesley, Reading, Mass.

Simon, H. A. (1969) *The Sciences of the Artificial*, MIT Press, Cambridge, Mass.

Smith, J. M. (1986) 'Expert database systems: a database perspective'. In Kerschberg, 1986.

Smith, J. M. and D. C. P. Smith (1977) 'Database abstractions: aggregation and generalisation', *ACM Transactions on Database Systems*, **2**(2), 105–33.

Sterling, L. and E. D. Shapiro (1986) *The Art of Prolog: Advanced Programming Techniques*, MIT Press, Cambridge, Mass.

Stonebraker, M. (1984a) 'Adding semantic knowledge to a relational database system'. In Brodie, 1984.

Stonebraker, M. (1984b) 'Triggers and inference in database systems'. In Brodie, 1984.

Stonebraker, M. (ed.) (1986) *The INGRES Papers*, Addison-Wesley, Reading, Mass.

Stonebraker, M. and M. Hearst (1989) 'Future trends in expert database systems'. In Kerschberg, 1989.

Stonebraker, M. and L. A. Rowe (1987a). *The Design of POSTGRES*, University of California, Berkeley, Electronics Research Laboratory, Internal Memorandum UCB/ERL 85/95.

Stonebraker, M. and L. A. Rowe (1987b) 'The POSTGRES data model', *Proc. VLDB Conference*, Brighton, 83–96.

Stonebraker, M., T. Sellis and E. Hanson (1986) 'An analysis of rule indexing implementations in data base systems'. In Kerschberg, 1986.

Storey, V. C. and R. C. Goldstein (1988) 'A methodology for creating user views in database design', *ACM Transactions on Database Systems*, **13**(3), 305–38.

Stow, R., S. Lunn and P. Slatter (1988) 'How to identify business applications of expert systems', *2nd International Expert Systems Conference*, Brighton.

Teorey, T. J., D. Yang and J. P. Fry (1986) 'A logical design methodology for relational databases using the extended entity–relationship model', *ACM Computing Surveys*, **18**, 197–222.

Tsitchizris, D. C. and F. H. Lochovsky (1982) *Data Models*, Prentice-Hall, Englewood Cliffs, N.J.

Ullman, J. D. (1988) *Principles of Database and Knowledge-base Systems* (Vol. 1), Computer Science Press, Rockville, Md.

Ullman, J. D. (1989) *Principles of Database and Knowledge-base Systems* (Vol. 2), Computer Science Press, Rockville, Md.

Van Melle, W., E. H. Shortliffe, B. G. Buchanan (1981) 'EMYCIN: a domain independent system that aids in constructing knowledge based consultation programs', *Machine Intelligence*, Infotech State of the Art Report 9, MIT Press, Mass.

Vassiliou, Y., J. Clifford and M. Jarke (1983) 'How does an expert system get its data?', *Proc. 9th Int. VLDB Conference*, Florence, 70–2.

Walker, A. (1984) 'Databases, expert systems, and PROLOG'. In Reitman, 1984.

Warner-Hasling, D. (1983) 'Abstract explanations of strategy in a diagnostic consultation system', *Proc. AAAI–83*, University of Maryland, William Kaufmann, Los Altos, Calif., 157–61.

Wasserman, A. I. and S. Gutz (1982) 'The future of programming', *Communications of ACM*, **25**(3), 196–206.

Webber, B. L. (1986) 'Natural language processing: a survey'. In Brodie *et al.*, 1984.

Weizenbaum, J. (1976) *Computer Power and Human Reason*, Freeman, San Francisco, Calif.

Wiederhold, G. (1984) 'Knowledge and database management', *IEEE Software*, January, 63–73.

Winston, P. H. (ed.) (1975) *The Psychology of Computer Vision*, McGraw-Hill, New York.

Winston, P. H. (1984) *Artificial Intelligence* (2nd edn), Addison-Wesley, Reading, Mass.

Winston, P. H. and K. A. Prendergast (eds) (1984) *The AI Business: the Commercial Uses of Artificial Intelligence*, MIT Press, Cambridge, Mass.

Yourdon, E. and L. L. Constantine (1979) *Structured Design: Fundamentals of a Discipline of Computer Program and System Design*, Prentice-Hall, Englewood Cliffs, N.J.

Suggested Solutions

Chapter 2

1. Four major properties:
   - (a) Program–data independence.
   - (b) Data integration.
   - (c) Data integrity.
   - (d) Separate logical and physical views of data.
2. A data model is an architecture for organizing data.
   - (a) Collection of data structures.
   - (b) Collection of operators.
   - (c) Collection of inherent integrity rules.
3. A relation is a disciplined table. It must adhere to a number of rules, e.g.:
   - (a) All columns must be assigned distinct names.
   - (b) All entries in a column must come from the same domain.
   - (c) Duplicate rows are not allowed.
   - (d) Each cell must be atomic.
   - (e) Ordering of columns and rows is not significant.
4. Entity and referential integrity are the inherent integrity rules of the relational data model.
   - (a) A table has entity integrity if it has a primary key.
   - (b) A table has referential integrity if all foreign key values either refer to a primary key value of another table or are null.

5.
```
CREATE TABLE employees (employee_no CHAR (2) NOT NULL,
                        name CHAR(10),
                        position CHAR(20),
                        salary NUM(6),
                        project_no CHAR(2))
```

6. (a)
```
SELECT *
FROM employees
WHERE name = 'Jones'
```

   (b)
```
SELECT number
FROM projects
```

   (c)
```
SELECT salary
FROM employees
WHERE employee_no = '04'
```

   (d)
```
SELECT name
FROM employees
WHERE project_no = (
    SELECT number
    FROM projects
    WHERE description = 'payroll')
```

(e) `SELECT number, AVG(salary)`
   `FROM projects, employees`
   `WHERE projects.number = employees.project_no`
   `GROUP BY number`

Chapter 3

1. (a) fact.
    (b) rule.
    (c) fact.
    (d) rule.
    (e) fact.
    (f) rule.
    (g) An interesting rule. A rule for handling other rules. A meta-rule.
3. A database has integrity if it is an accurate reflection of some subset of the real world.
4. Inherent means part of the architectural definition of the data model. Mechanisms should be available in any relational DBMS for enforcing entity and referential integrity.
5.
```
CREATE TABLE employees (employee_no CHAR (2)
                        name CHAR(10),
                        position CHAR(20),
                        salary NUM(6),
                        project_no CHAR(2))
PRIMARY KEY (employee_no)
FOREIGN KEY (project_no IDENTIFIES projects.number,
             DELETE OF project_no RESTRICTED,
             UPDATE OF projects.number CASCADES)
```
6.
```
CREATE ASSERTION a3
    ON projects
    DEFINE FORALL projects (
           EXISTS EMPLOYEES (projects.number =
                             employees.project_no AND
                             employees.position =
                             'project manager'))
```
7.
```
CREATE TRIGGER T2
    ON INSERT OF employees
    UPDATE projects
    SET employee_total = employee_total + 1
    WHERE employees.project_no = projects.number
```
8.
```
CREATE ALERTER R2
ON UPDATE OF employees
ALERT stevens
```

Chapter 4

1. In traditional terms a database is a mechanism for storing a large collection of isolated facts, a knowledge base is a mechanism for

storing a potentially large collection of rules. We have used knowledge base in this work however in a more encompassing sense as a fact base and a rule base.

2. A knowledge base system is a more encompassing term than expert system. There are some knowledge base systems that would not be regarded as an expert system *per se*. For instance, a natural language system is a knowledge base system.

3. (a) rule base
   (b) working memory
   (c) inference engine
   (d) user interface.

4. An expert system shell is a tool for building expert systems. It is an expert system devoid of domain-specific knowledge.

5. (a) diagnosis
   (b) planning
   (c) prediction, etc.

6. (a) production rules
   (b) logic
   (c) frames
   (d) semantic nets.

7. In a forward chaining mechanism inference moves forward from data stored in working memory to the goal to be solved. The system does this by attempting to match the facts stored in WM against the conditions or IF parts of the rules in the knowledge base. Forward chaining is often referred to as data-directed reasoning. In a backward chaining system the user normally selects a goal for the system to solve. The inference mechanism then attempts to solve this goal by searching through the knowledge base for a rule which has an identifier in its conclusion, or THEN part, which matches the identifier in the goal. Backward chaining is hence often referred to as goal-directed chaining.

8. The process of undoing an unproductive inference and exploring alternatives.

9. Conflict resolution corresponds to the inference mechanism making up its mind which rule to fire from a set of potential rules in any one cycle of inference.
   Conflict resolution strategies:
   (a) prioritization of rules
   (b) rule-base recency
   (c) working memory recency
   (d) specificity.

10. People are able to explain aspects of their behaviour. If expert

systems are meant to simulate at least certain aspects of human behaviour then these artefacts should also be able to explain their reasoning. This is particularly true if the user of such systems is to feel confident of their reasoning.

Chapter 5

1. An evolutionary approach to a KBMS represents the exploitation of existing tools and techniques such as expert system shells and database management systems. In contrast, a revolutionary approach would need to propose an alternative, radical architecture which is able to encompass both rule-like and fact-like knowledge.
2. (a)   an enhanced database system or enhanced expert system
   (b)   an enhanced database system
   (c)   an enhanced expert system.
3. An expert system was built for this task. The expert system was aimed at enabling building society customers, with the aid of trained staff, to get some reasonable idea of the worth of a particular property prior to making a formal mortgage application. This enables building societies to filter out at an early stage all those properties clearly over-priced in terms of their agreed purchase price. Customers are saved the expense of a valuation survey, and the building society saves the effort involved in a potentially unfruitful application.
4. Stow describes unstructured decision-making areas as being the most suitable for expert system development. Certain structured areas such as car insurance broking, however, may be suitable because of the convenience of the expert systems approach.

Chapter 6

1.
```
ALWAYS REPLACE employees(working_week = 40
                   AND salary = 80)
WHERE employees.dept = 'production'
      employees.type = 'shop_floor'
```
2. This RPL statement simulates, in a forward chaining manner, the small credit assessment rule base described in Chapter 4.
3. Only (c) is parsable.
4. Management information systems. End-user enquiry of a company database.
5. That mechanism within any relational DBMS which decides on the

optimal way to implement a query in terms of primitive database operations. One way of thinking of the work of a query optimizer is as a mechanism which maps nonprocedural statements expressed in a language such as SQL into a procedural implementation in something like the relational algebra.

6. Specific rules written into the database may cut down on the amount of data that needs to be stored. One disadvantage is that there is an obvious processing overhead to semantic optimization.

Chapter 7

1. The degree of coupling refers to the interconnectedness of expert system to database system. A weakly coupled system is one in which connection is at the periphery. A file of data is read prior to expert system execution or a file of data is written after execution. Loose and tight coupling refers to direct communication between expert system and database during execution.

2. Weak coupling.

3. SQL select statements might be called from the conditions of rules. SQL update, insert or delete statements might be fired from conclusions. For example,

```
IF customer is (run customer.sql) SELECT command
       ...
THEN run cins.sql     INSERT commands
```

4. ```
Customers(customer_no, name, address, branch_no,
              date_of_birth, employment_status,
              company_scheme, serps, security)
```

# Chapter 8

1. (a) Flexibility.
   (b) Efficiency.
   (c) Versatility.
   (d) Functionality.

2. A system catalogue is a meta-database—a database of information about base data. The data dictionary discussed in this chapter stores information not only about base data, but also the interrelationships between data items and knowledge items.

3. The personal pension adviser could run as a stand-alone expert system, in which case the operator would need to re-run the system for each customer application. In contrast, the expert system could
```

take its input from a file of previously entered customer applications. In this mode the expert system could run with little operator intervention.
4. Any changes to the expert system will need to be reflected in the data dictionary and perhaps even in the structure of the database. Likewise, any changes to the structure of the database need to be checked off against the data dictionary and associated expert systems.

Chapter 9

1. A data-model which uses richer and more expressive concepts to capture real-world meaning than is possible using classic data models such as the relational data model.
2. Aggregation is the process of using a higher-level object to group together a number of lower-level objects. Association is the process of specifying a relationship between objects which builds a higher-level object.
3. The relational data model is a minimal data model. It has no direct mechanisms, for instance, for modelling generalization and the process of inheritance.
4. This rule defines what it means to be a major supplier. That is, a supplier who supplies more than 30000 items of a given part.
5. (a) Greater economy of expression—at least from the user's point of view.
   (b) More explicit mechanisms for integrity maintenance.
   (c) The ability to model data in more than one way.
   (d) More efficient modelling of user concepts.

Chapter 10

1. Frame: EMPLOYEE
        Name: unit(surname, forename)
        Age: unit(years)
        Address: unit(number, street, town, county)
        Salary: unit(pounds)
        Start-date: unit(month, year)
        Department: unit(name)

Frame: MANAGER
        AKO: EMPLOYEE
        Staffing: unit(integer)

Frame: TECHNICIAN
AKO: EMPLOYEE

Technician__grade: unit(integer)
Technical__allowance: unit(pounds)

Frame: SECRETARY
AKO: EMPLOYEE
Secretarial__grade: unit(integer)
Secretarial__allowance: unit(pounds)

Frame: M1
Is-A: MANAGER
Name: Beynon-Davies, Paul
Age: 30
Address: 38 Nowhere Rd, Llantrisant, Mid-Glam.
Salary: 20 000
Start-date: April, 1972
Department: Marketing
Staffing: 12

Frame: T1
Is-A: TECHNICIAN
Name: Smith, Phil
Age: 24
Address: 50 Dumfries Place, Cardiff, Mid-Glam.
Salary: 10 000
Start-date: April, 1980
Department: Computing
Technical__grade: 12
Technical__allowance: 1000

Frame: S1
Is-A: SECRETARY
Name: Knowall, Angela
Age: 24
Address: 40 Erewhon Place, Newport, Mid-Glam.
Salary: 8000
Start-date: April, 1985
Department: Marketing
Secretarial__grade: 2
Secretarial__allowance: 500

2. A difficult distinction to make. One possibility is to describe semantic data models as mechanisms which attempt to provide structural

abstractions. Object-oriented models are geared more towards behavioural abstractions. Semantic models are oriented towards the representation of data while object-oriented models are concerned more with the manipulation of data.

3.
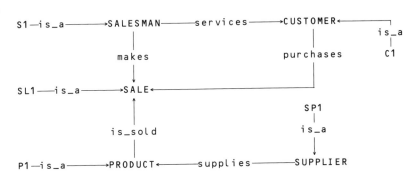

4. 'A kind of' links sub-types to types. 'Is a' links instances to types.
5. Similarities:
    (a) A basic frame is roughly equivalent to a row in a relation.
    (b) A slot is roughly equivalent to an attribute of a relation.
    Differences:
    (a) Frames are a far more complex construct than relations. For example, slots can contain a lot more than simple data values.
    (b) Relations are deterministic, frames non-deterministic.
6. (a) Ability to define complex objects.
    (b) Ability to define procedures associated with objects.
    (c) Ability to distinguish between two objects with the same characteristics.

Chapter 11

1. Predicate calculus consists of:
    A set of constants;
    A set of variables;
    A set of predicates, each taking a specified number of arguments;
    The logical connectives;
    The existential and universal quantifiers;
    A set of inference rules.
2. director(davies, simplesoft)
    works_for(jones, simplesoft)
    works_for(evans, simplesoft)
    analyst_programmer(jones)

analyst__programmer(evans)

hardware__expert(jones)

3. Because there are too many rules of inference. We cannot determine algorithmically which rule of inference to apply next in a sequence.

4. (a) Each account belongs to single customer.
   (b) Every customer has at least one account.
   (c) No customer has more than four accounts.
   (d) The sum of the balances of all the accounts held by a customer must not exceed the customer's total maximum balance.

5. (a) ∀ l ∈ LIFE_POLICY
       ∃ p ∈ POLICY WHERE
        p.policy_no = l.policy_no
   (b) ∀ v ∈ VEHICLE_POLICY
       ∃ p ∈ POLICY WHERE
        p.policy_no = v.policy_no
   (c) ∀ p ∈ POLICY
       (∃ l ∈ LIFE_POLICY WHERE
        p.policy_no = l.policy_no)
     OR
       (∃ v ∈ VEHICLE_POLICY_WHERE
        p.policy_no = v.policy_no)
   (d) ∀ l ∈ LIFE_POLICY
      NOT ∃ v ∈ VEHICLE_POLICY WHERE
        l.policy_no = v.policy_no

6. c(bloggs, 200).
   c(bilbo, 150).
   c(baggins, 250).

   a(0101, 10, bloggs).
   a(0102, 20, bloggs).
   a(0201, 100, bilbo).
   a(0202, 75, bilbo).
   a(0301, 200, baggins).

7. No, the accounts for bilbo infringe constraint 4(d).

Chapter 12

1.

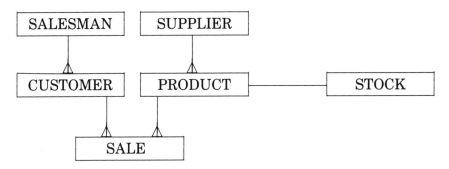

2. (a) Basic E–R diagram cannot represent inheritance.
   (b) E–R diagram does not indicate instances of entities/objects.
   (c) E–R diagram documents degrees of relationships.
3. (a) $1{:}M$ (b) $M{:}N$ (c) $M{:}N$
4. Because the E–R model has the ability to express more real-world semantics, particularly in the area of integrity constraints.
5. Rules expressed in POSTQUEL would be able to build and modify elements of a system catalogue.
6. (a) Location transparency
   (b) data fragmentation
   (c) fragmentation transparency
   (d) data replication.
7. A distributed database system is homogeneous if the same DBMS is running on various machines in the network. A DDB is heterogeneous if a number of different DBMSs are running. A federated database system is one in which each node in the network is an autonomous unit, but each node is also able to cooperate with other nodes to build a distributed database scheme.

Index